MW01118400

TORN BETWEEN
TWO WORLDS

MODERN MEDICINE AND
SPIRITUAL HEALING

SHAWN T MURPHY

BALBOA.PRESS
A DIVISION OF HAY HOUSE

Balboa Press books may be ordered through booksellers or by contacting:

Balboa Press
A Division of Hay House
1663 Liberty Drive
Bloomington, IN 47403
www.balboapress.com
844-682-1282

Print information available on the last page.

ISBN: 978-1-9822-7002-5 (sc)
ISBN: 978-1-9822-7005-6 (hc)
ISBN: 978-1-9822-7001-8 (e)

Library of Congress Control Number: 2021911949

Balboa Press rev. date: 08/26/2021

This book is dedicated
to Mary Ann and those like you;
may your new journey begin.
It is equally dedicated to
Kimberley Mendrono and all
those whose journey ended
prematurely in spiritual battle.

CONTENTS

INTRODUCTION

IN THE FIRST THREE BOOKS of *Torn Between Two Worlds* I recount the historical events that destroyed the holistic worldview once held by the Ionian Greeks[1]—a society from which great wisdom sprang. It has also been a source of inspiration when modern society has come to an impasse. Galileo returned there to start the scientific renaissance. Erwin Schrödinger returned to this wisdom at the dawn of quantum mechanics to discover where science had gone astray. Dr. Edward Bach returned to the teachings of the father of the Hippocratic Oath to find where modern medicine had gone astray.

This book is dedicated to furthering the investigation that Dr. Bach initiated and providing more tools in the pursuit of *healing thyself*. This requires embarking on a journey similar to one that Dr. Bach took. I started my journey with the *Torn Between Two Worlds* trilogy where I developed three theories uniting the origins of science and origins of religion and uncovering the rhetoric that has driven a wedge between them. The central theory from this project is the *two-world hypothesis*:

We are citizens of two coincidental worlds; a physical world, which is open to the eyes of its inhabitants, and an ethereal world only visible to a few gifted individuals. The physical world is finite, in which it is limited to the materials created in the Big Bang, whereas the ethereal world is infinite. Both worlds can act upon each other.

Why is this knowledge so important in the field of medicine and our pursuit of healing ourselves? Sickness, and especially mental illness, can be caused by a physiological process or a spiritual process, or a combination of both. For example, when the American Medical Association (AMA) only approves treatments for the physical body, the spirit can continue to suffer when the root cause turns out to be of spiritual origin. Regardless of

---

[1] See Appendix 4: A return to the high ethic of the Ionian Ideal.

the "major advances" made in medicine, many people still suffer spiritual illnesses, even when they have access to "quality health care."

I have three personal examples of where "medically approved" procedures were not the solution for the symptoms my family members were experiencing. In all three cases, prescription drugs were used to treat the spiritual ailments of depression, anxiety, and attention deficit disorder in three different family members.

- The medication for depression that my sibling was prescribed did not stop three suicide attempts, nor was it responsible for the eventual spiritual cure of the cause of the depression.
- The family member with anxiety became addicted to the medications prescribed to treat the illness. The medication temporally treated the symptoms, but it exposed a second symptom from the underlying cause. In the end, anxiety was conquered not as a result of the medication initially prescribed but through finding purpose in life.
- In the third case, the drugs prescribed led to years of experimentation with many illegal drugs in search of a "better way of thinking." Eventually, they realized that there was nothing wrong with the way they thought, it was just different than the way others wanted them to think. The only thing "wrong" in the beginning was a very inquisitive mind.

In all three cases, treating the physical body not only failed to address the underlying spiritual condition, it resulted in decades of suffering by delaying the eventual treatment of the underlying cause of their ailment. I have witnessed the impact of neglecting the ethereal world, including some of my closest family members. I have been fortunate to have recognized these dangers and I have been able to protect myself and my immediate family from them to some extent. But I have less luck with close friends.

I had a dear friend with whom I had many spiritual discussions during his life. I knew him for over twenty-five years. He spent his life searching for the truth and studied all the philosophers and religions. He introduced me to my wife and to the knowledge he had gained in his lifelong search. Even though I respected his knowledge and caring for others, I recognized in him an arrogance that I was uncomfortable with. He was fanatical when it came to his belief. I say this with all respect. I had tried to make him aware of this shortcoming but was unable to steer him from his fanatical path.

He had been married twice and lost his second wife to breast cancer. She was a lovely woman, but she suffered with him. He had three daughters and no sons. I recognized this as his fate, because he was unable to respect women, so he was fated to be surrounded by them. As long as I knew him, he said he could not wait to get to heaven. It came up in every discussion I had with him during the past twenty-five years. Each time he said it, it pained me, and I usually reminded him that his father lived to be old.

He died last year, after deciding not to treat his kidney failure. He left his house to his youngest daughter, who is our godchild. Shortly after he died, strange things started to occur in her house. It was clear his spirit was not content.

This is what we found out about his arrival in heaven. He had been looking forward to being greeted by his guardian angel for many years, but when he arrived, his guardian had a grim face. He was not pleased! Expecting to be greeted by his deceased wife, he was shocked to discover that she took one look and walked away without saying a word. He was brought to the place in heaven that he had earned, and he was unhappy with the accommodations and the job he was given. Every time he could muster up his free will, he would escape back to his house and let out his frustrations on his daughter.

This is one of the saddest stories that I personally know, but it is not an unusual occurrence. When religious fanatics get to heaven, they are met with something different from what they expect, often return to their old haunts, and can cause their family members prolonged suffering.

This book is dedicated to those who have had similar misfortunes and is written in hopes of shortening the suffering of those who are currently being treated only for their physical symptoms. Its goal is to show how the ethereal world can negatively impact our daily lives and to open the eyes of those who do not recognize we are each a dualistic being—a human body and a coincidental spiritual body with its soul. Gaining understanding of the dangers from the ethereal world and applying our collective knowledge to overcome these dangers would greatly benefit society in general, especially those suffering from unrecognized sources.

The work of Dr. Edward Bach, *Heal Thyself*, guides this book, as it helps you, the reader, to utilize the knowledge of yourself to discover the root spiritual cause of your ailment. The book then provides strategies for addressing the root causes that can be of use immediately. This book is not a replacement for a practitioner—a surgeon, cardiologist, or psychologist—but rather a guide to find the most suitable allies in effectively treating your condition or a loved one's condition.

In the first half of this book, I explain the diversity of spiritual ailments that can cause human suffering, before moving on to recommending strategies to address them in the second half of the book.

CHAPTER 1

A Primer on Possession

A great many mental problems result from intervention by spirits. The most prevalent is lack of concentration— "fuzzing out," as one patient put it. Another said, "My mind takes little breaks—like skipping a spot for a while," and "Part shuts off—Blanksville!" Memory problems, like forgetting something done or said, missing exits on the freeway, etc., are typical. In my practice I find occasional "forgetting" of therapy appointments often reflects the spirit's resistance to dispossession. This is especially evident when we have been working with recalcitrant entities.

The reason forgetting is a problem is that there are two or even more people inhabiting the same body, all "doing their own thing" from time to time. The possessing spirit may decide he wants ice cream, and the patient "comes to" with her hand on the freezer door and can't remember why she's opening it. This, of course, depends on how the two are interacting. If one takes over and the other phases out, then that kind of behavior is experienced. In other cases, the thoughts of the spirit's mind are picked up and acted upon by the possessed with no break in consciousness. — Dr. Edith Fiore[2]

THE FAMILIAR TOPIC OF POSSESSION, while well-known, does not seem to be well understood. There is often much superstition around this topic and many charged feelings when discussing it as a possible cause for

---

[2] Edith Fiore, "The Effects of Possession," *The Unquiet Dead: a Psychologist Treats Spirit Possession* (Ballantine Books, 1991), 38.

psychosis. I am not saying that possession causes all psychosis but rather that psychosis can be a symptom of possession where the only effective cure is through spiritual means.

To start with, I examine the variety of spiritual entities that may want to possess a human and their motives. Then I investigate the diversity of impact they can have on our lives. Finally, I examine the spiritual laws governing their interactions, which will guide us in determining effective treatments and defenses.

Possession is much more frequent than many believe because relative to the stereotype, the symptoms are much more benign. The outward symptoms of possession can appear as simple forgetfulness or indecisiveness. The inner, spiritual conflict is not readily observable, but it exists. I will begin with the harsh cases of possession and work backward to the most subtle.

Evil Spirits

One winter day ten years later, when Mrs. Wickland and I were alone in our home in Chicago, Mrs. Wickland was unexpectedly controlled by a spirit who gasped for breath and seemed to be strangling. This spirit, like so many others, was unconscious of controlling a body not its own, and upon contacting matter, again experienced its last death struggle.

After much questioning I learned, to my great surprise, that this was the spirit of my former friend, who had ended her physical life by hanging herself. She was still bound to the earth sphere and related the indescribable mental hell she had been in during all those years.

"As soon as I found myself out of my body, I saw at once the cause for my rash act. Evil spirits, who had been attracted to me by the jealous thoughts of other persons, were standing near, grinning with devilish satisfaction at their work.

"They had influenced me to end my life; I had no occasion to even think of such folly. An irresistible impulse had suddenly come over me. I fastened the rope around my neck, and only realized what I had done when it was too late.

"I would have given the world to have been able to regain possession of my body. Oh, what horrors of despair and remorse I have gone through! My home shattered, my husband brokenhearted and discouraged, and my little ones needing my care!"[3]

The classic portrayal of possession by evil spirits comes from the movie *The Exorcist*, and it has brought much rhetoric into the topic that needs to be clarified. First of all, there is a major difference between Old Testament times and New Testament times. In the time of Jesus, for example, we read of legions of evil spirits possessing people and animals. Up until the time of Jesus's victory over Satan, evil spirits were unlimited—they could possess anyone that they wanted. After Jesus passed Final Judgment[4] over the ruler of this world, evil spirits are only allowed to possess those who willingly give themselves over to evil.

A person who is possessed by an evil spirit has made a commitment to evil; therefore, an exorcism is futile. Without changing their allegiance, another evil spirit would simply return after the exorcism as long as the open invitation exists. The legends of vampires have their basis in these spiritual facts. Once you invite them in, it is challenging to keep them out.

The other misnomer of possession by an evil spirit is that the possessed person acts evil. The proper description would be narcissistic, but even that is too simplistic. There are various motivations that evil pursues in this world, most of which are not obviously evil. The number-one goal of evil is to lead people away from the original teachings of Jesus and the prophets. Their success is significant, when we look at the organizations that proclaim

[3] Carl August Wickland, "Spirits and Suicide," *30 Years among the Dead* (Borgo Press, 1980), 109.
[4] See Appendix 1: Final Judgment.

to represent Jesus. This was accomplished with superb fineness and through well-laid plans. For instance, many people today refer to Constantine as "the great," while he was the key instigator turning early Christianity into a pagan, materialistic religion. The long-term impact of his clever moves fragmented this religion into thousands of sects. By dividing Christianity this way, evil effectively conquered the most powerful tool available to defeat it. The pagan Romans left the world with the doctrines of the trinity[5] and of eternal damnation[6] and plunged the West into the Dark Ages with a complete absence of en*Light*enment.

Needless to say, evil spirits need a willing participant, someone susceptible to visions of fame, power, wealth, or other material pleasantry. There is not much we can do for those who choose to be possessed by an evil spirit. We need to concentrate our efforts on how to recognize their presence and how to protect ourselves from people who have given in to evil. We can also create strategies to limit their impact.

The other major role evil spirits play is cheerleading, as we see from the quotation from Dr. Wickland at the beginning of this section. Evil spirits actively encourage those with questionable morals or ethics by giving them a "warm feeling" when they get away with a lie, steal something, or abuse someone. This is one way for evil spirits to indirectly attack people of good intent. Since they are protected by a faithful guardian spirit from a direct assault, an evil spirit will instead find allies in weak-willed or amoral people in the circle of friends or family of their target. Evil finds the weakest link in the close circle and exploits it. One more reason why we need to pray in earnest for "the least of our brothers/sisters."

Evil spirits can whisper to people at their weakest moments and take advantage of their vulnerability. This is not possession per se, but they would much rather talk someone into killing themselves instead of possessing them. Thankfully, there is much that we can do to limit their impact on our lives and those close to us. These strategies are laid out in chapters 11 and 12.

---

[5] Robert Sträuli, "Das Konzil von Nicaea," *Origenes, Der Diamantene* (ABZ-Verl., 1987), 159–162.

[6] See Appendix 2: Origen of Alexandria, a prophet?

Demons

> An evil spirit and a demon are not the same. A demon forms from the evil thoughts of man. But it is lifeless, that is to say, it is without willpower, it has nothing active in itself, these are shapes, lifeless forms. (Lene)[7]

Lene is a divine spiritual teacher who lectured at GL Zürich for over thirty years through deep-trance medium Beatrice Brunner. Her 60-to-90-minute lectures have all been recorded and transcribed in print. They are available to read at glz.org. I refer to Lene's lectures in this book when I have found no other expert on the given subject matter, as she provides a unique perspective from the highest regions of the spiritual world.

The terms *evil spirit* and *demon* are often used synonymously, but for the purposes of my work, I want to clearly distinguish between them. Demons are raw, negative energy generated from people. They can be formed from one person or multiple people's thoughts of envy, jealousy, hate, anger, or vengeance. This demon can possess a person, amplifying their own negative character. There is no additional personality or will driving the person, but demons can be formidable. This type of demon possession can cause a person to snap at a loved one or even drive a person to murder, giving the possessed enough negative energy to fulfill a deeply held negative wish.

Vengeful Spirits

> In my wanderings upon the earth plane I have learned many ways in which a spirit can still work mischief to those he hates who are yet in the flesh. Far more power is ours than you would dream of, but I feel it is wiser to let the veil rest still upon the possibilities the world holds even after death for the revengeful spirit. I could detail many terrible cases I know of as having actually taken place—mysterious murders and strange crimes committed, none knew why or

---

[7] "Seele, Geist und Körper," *Geistige Welt* 2018, no. 3: 9 (Translated from the German by Google).

how, by those on earth whose brains were so disordered that they were not themselves responsible for their actions, and were but the tools of a possessing spirit. These and many kindred things are known to us in the spirit spheres where circumstances often wear a very different aspect from the one shown to you. The old beliefs in demoniacal possession were not so visionary after all, only these demons or devils had themselves been once the denizens of earth.[8]

More common than evil spirits are vengeful spirits. These are spirits of people with whom we have unresolved conflicts, either from this lifetime or from a previous lifetime. These spirits have not forgiven us for wronging them and continue to seek vengeance from us in their afterlife.

The most severe cases of schizophrenia and dissociative identity disorder can be caused by multiple vengeful spirits fighting for control over a person's body while tormenting their spirit. There are two ways to stop the cycle of vengeance. The first is through forgiveness, and it must be on both sides. As long as one party is unwilling to forgive the other, the cycle continues. The second way to resolve this cycle is through the process of *repaying our debts*. These unresolved conflicts, therefore, can play out over multiple lifetimes. That is why I call it "the Gift of Reincarnation"[9] because it is a process that allows us all to resolve these conflicts the hard way, through suffering.

Lost Spirits

So the guests came, one after the other, and people began to talk and argue with one another. They also talked about this Karrer [a nickname given to a man with a handcart], who had now died. He wasn't talked about very nicely. He had to listen to such things. He got angry and knocked his fist on the table. To do this, he used that person's hand. This person was now obsessed with him and had

---

[8] A. Farnese, "Chapter 8 – Temptation," *Wanderer in the Spirit Lands* (Franchezzo), 20.
[9] See Appendix 3.

the same bad habits as the Karrer had had in his human life. Suddenly this man, who normally took his drink but knew the limits, began to drink too much; he no longer knew the limits.

The Karrer liked that, because now it was he who ruled these people. When it got late, this guest, who was meanwhile quite drunk, was asked to go home at last. When he left, the Karrer—that is, his ghost—stayed behind in this tavern or restaurant. Then he saw other spirits who were also staying in this restaurant. They started talking to him, praising him and complimenting him. They praised him for how he had lived; that he really had something out of his life and savored it; that he would have been one of the sensible ones and that he would have had a good time in this restaurant. He could live here as long as he wanted. It was lower spirits talking to him. They looked just as bad as he did. He agreed with them and felt apt with his own kind. So it went on evening after evening: again and again he pounced on the first guest who came into this dining room; he began to master this. So there was always a quarrel in this restaurant, because if he could take possession of a person, he let off steam. Behind and next to him he now saw these gloomy spirits who persuaded him and encouraged him to live even further, even more in this way. He felt satisfied here because he could live it out as he pleased. (Lene)[10]

This category of possessing spirits is troublesome indeed. They are not actual evil spirits, and they do not have to be familiar spirits, but they do share a special bond with their victims: addiction. When a person dies, their spirit lives on in the afterlife on the same trajectory that they lived as a human. Contrary to some teachers, the soul or spirit does not become enlightened upon death or become one with a universal pure soul. They do not become

---

[10] Lene, "Vom Kampf zwischen Gut und Böse," *Meditationswoche 1970*, by Beatrice Brunner, GL Zürich, 2020, pp. 78–79 (Translated from the German by Google).

all-knowing or virtuous. Their spirit has the same level of (un)enlightenment as they did as a human. They have the same virtues or lack thereof.

So, when a materialistic person with addiction dies, their spirit lives on in the afterlife with the same addiction and the same personality. They still crave the same behavior they had as humans. They prey on those people with similar desires so that they can satisfy their addictions through others. As stated in the quoted text above, there are plenty of cheerleaders in the afterlife to praise their unvirtuous behavior that they may not have received from their friends or family members. Their "talents" are finally recognized, and they have no reason to change the "good life" they have found. These types of spirits can prey on addicted people for hundreds of years.

Familiar Spirits

> An amusing example comes to mind. In the beginning of her treatment, Marilyn released a few entities: her dominating mother and other relatives. In a later session, she sheepishly confessed she had been wrestling with an important decision and had called upon spirits to help her, even though she was aware of the potential dangers. She laughed and said, "So many chimed in with their opinions—I had a committee— all disagreeing!" We discovered that a few had stayed with her, as she had suspected.

> A phenomenon not generally understood is the invisible or imaginary playmate. Under hypnosis, it's been clear to my patients that these were actually spirits. Close bonds of friendship and a dependency at one point resulted in a merging of the two, the spirit and the child. From then on, they cohabited the body and the possessed was consciously unaware of the possession.[11]

---

[11] Edith Fiore, "Spirit Entry," *The Unquiet Dead: a Psychologist Treats Spirit Possession* (Ballantine Books, 1991), 115–116.

This may be the most common form of possession, and, simultaneously, the most insidious. It is the most common because so many people long for their loved ones who have passed. It is this longing that allows these spirits of the dead to linger instead of moving on with their afterlife. In addition, these spirits want to comfort those they left behind, and they believe that by staying, they can do this.

This codependency makes it insidious since neither wants to break the bond. But being cooped up in one body with your relatives over the long run is unhealthy. Even the healthiest relationship of this type can lead to neurosis, with multiple sentient beings exerting their will on the mind and body simultaneously.

It is important to know that all the above can be at play simultaneously. Fortunately, we have access to the works of many clairvoyants who can illustrate this for those of us who do not have this spiritual gift. The following excerpt from *Die entschleierte Aura* shows how many forces can be at play when a person has opened themselves up to the influence of others.

Etheric body with mediumistic obsession[12]

The odic aura of this medium is pink-red. The seer recognizes from the changed tint that the woman is being directed by someone else's will. This is also made clear by the hand that has penetrated the aura, which belongs to the astral body of the human being, which misuses the medium for its own purposes. The pale color of the etheric body shows the weakening of health through this external influence. The radiation of the living fluid is also disturbed and only partially available. On the right behind the head of the etheric body one sees the head of the astral body of the woman, on the left the head and hand of a deceased, earthbound man. The aura has got a crack through repeated hypnotization at the top left, the astral body of the medium was pushed out by the hypnotist at the upper part, and this enabled the astral body of the deceased to penetrate.

The medium is not under direct hypnosis, but nevertheless receives the will and power of the hypnotist, as does the body of the deceased, because the hypnotist enables him to withdraw life force from the etheric body of the medium. The devilish demonic [evil spirit] being takes physical strength from the possessed and also damages their other bodies. As a result, she is inhibited in her spiritual development until she has freed herself from the spirit of possession and the demon on her own with the help of beings who serve God, and this can occasionally require many lives. It depends on how much she lets herself be abused through her own fault and how quickly she can free herself from the entanglement of evil through her own efforts.

Entering such an obsession can seem harmless. It can be one or more hypnotic treatments for health reasons or because of mental disorders, as well as an activity as a spiritualistic medium or visitor to such a session, if the person has the prerequisites for an obsession. But it can also be all other media abilities that have arisen through astral or mental external influence and not through inspiration from higher beings. This includes, for example, artistic activities of all kinds that the otherwise inartistic person has to perform compulsively. It is different when people are inspired by higher

---

[12] Gisela Weigl and Franz Wenzel, *Die entschleierte Aura*, 2nd ed. (Aquamarin, 1986), 49–51, 116 (Translated from the German by Google).

beings. This voluntary cooperation takes place in waking consciousness or a higher state of consciousness, which is to be called divine. People who receive this are characterized by great humility and are not interested in fame and material possessions. They feel like earthly tools in the hand of God and do their spiritual work for the good of their fellow brothers and sisters with selfless devotion. As long as they stay true to this path, without being confused or seduced by external appearances, they will never suffer any damage to health or mentality. However, this is the case with media inclined people who go this way out of curiosity, folly or greed for money or even deliberately mislead and harm other people. Only man goes the right and safe path, who places himself completely under God and is a true friend and brother to all his fellow creatures. When he has the necessary maturity, he will gradually develop all these abilities which belong to his perfection and which he places entirely at the service of his brothers and sisters from all areas of nature. He will never harm any creature, no matter how minor, through his talent, neither materially, mentally, nor spiritually, because for him they are all his younger and older siblings in spirit.

CHAPTER 2

Past-Life Trauma

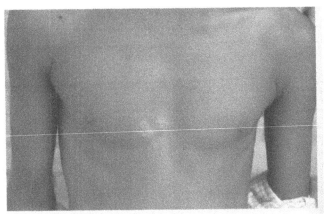

Figure 6 Birthmark on Hanumant Saxena's chest as it appeared in 1971, when he was 16 years old. The birthmark was an area of lessened pigmentation.

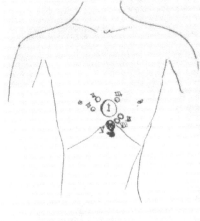

Figure 7 Sketch showing location of fatal wounds on Maha Ram Singh. Dr. S. C. Pandeya (Civil Surgeon, Fatehgarh, U.P., India) drew the circles on the lower chest and upper abdomen. The Roman numerals correspond to the different wounds described in the autopsy report. Number I was the largest wound. Note the characteristic smaller wounds on the periphery of the large, central wound. This is due to the scattering of the shot after they leave the barrel of the gun.

Hanumant's birthmark corresponded closely in location to the fatal wound on Maha Ram, and I shall say a little about him and how he died. Maha Ram was born in about 1905 in the same village as Hanumant, and his house was not more than 250 meters from that of Hanumant's family. He was a farmer who had some land and owned a bullock-cart, which he sometimes drove for hire. He married and had five children. His younger brother described him as a "simple, good fellow". He had no known enemies. Nevertheless, on the evening of September 28, 1954, he was standing near a teashop at the crossroads, not far from his home, when someone shot him at close range with a shotgun. He died almost immediately. His assailant fled, and because he had not been identified, the police made no arrests. Because Maha Ram was such a harmless person, he might have been killed accidentally, his murderer, in the dark, having mistaken him for someone else.

The postmortem report showed that the main charge of pellets had hit Maha Ram in the lower chest in the midline; there was some scattering of wounds from shot around the principal wound. The Indian doctor who examined the postmortem report with me (and who had no knowledge of the location of Hanumant's birthmark) sketched in the location of wounds on a human figure drawing (Figure 7). This shows the almost exact correspondence between the wounds and Hanumant's birthmark.

Hanumant began to speak when he was about 1 year old. When he was about 3 years old, he started referring to the life of Maha Ram. He said that he was Maha Ram, and, pointing to his birthmark, he said that he had been shot there. He made a few other statements that were correct for Maha Ram, and he recognized some people and places familiar to Maha Ram. In particular, he recognized Maha

Ram's bullocks, which was perhaps not difficult because
the bullocks were standing outside Maha Ram's house.[13]

THE TIRELESS RESEARCH OF DR. Ian Stevenson and Dr. Jim
Tucker at the University of Virginia provides strong evidence of the
Two-World Hypothesis—physical injury can damage the spirit, and
an injured spirit incarnating into a newborn can damage the newborn
physical body. This barely scratches the surface of the possible past-
life traumas that we can bring into our present lifetime. Besides
the physical trauma that leaves a physical imprint on the newborn,
other spiritual injuries can be carried into a new lifetime as mental trauma.

I shared this research with a close friend of mine and halfway through
my explanation she took off her shirt and pointed to the birthmark in the
middle of her chest. Putting her shirt back on, she explained to me her
medical history. Since early childhood she had suffered from back pain.
The pain was centered in her spine, opposite the birthmark on her chest.
She also had an unexplained, deathly fear of handguns, not guns in general
or rifles, but only handguns.

She explained the journey she took in her attempt to eliminate her back
pain, and not until her mid-thirties did she find a spiritual healer who put
the pieces together. The back pain was directly behind the birthmark in
her chest and centered where the bullet was lodged in the spine and killed
her in her previous lifetime. MRIs never showed any damage to her back
that could account for the pain, but the spiritual healer sensed insufficient
energy in this part of her spine. The injury to her spirit in the past life had
not healed, bringing pain into this body where the deadly bullet had lodged
in her spine. The healing of this spiritual injury in her spine also cured her
phobia of handguns. The phobia was the trauma associated with this past-
life injury.

Past-life trauma can cause phobias in this lifetime. Someone who died in an
airplane crash in the past life could easily display a fear of flying in this life.

---

[13] Ian Stevenson, "Verification of Wounds by Medical Records," *Where Reincarnation
and Biology Intersect*, by (Praeger, 1997), 50, figures 6 and 7.

Fear of heights could be from a death due to a fall in the past life and fear of driving from dying in a car accident. A fear of the water can be caused by drowning in the previous life; germophobia can be a result of dying of disease. It is often difficult for some to have empathy with those suffering from phobias because many die a natural death and not a traumatic death. Therefore, not everyone lives with this type of past-life phobia.

These are the obvious or logical past-life traumas, which one can bring into a new lifetime, that are easily traceable to a past-life event. But there are other, more subtle traumas that we can carry. These are the interpersonal conflicts that we create and bring with us into the current lifetime. These spiritual conflicts transcend the material world. When we die in conflict with others, they mostly remain unresolved, and they can only be fully resolved in the physical world. Since we are not altogether conscious of these unresolved conflicts, we can continue to unconsciously harbor hate or jealousy through our lifetime without seeking resolution or forgiveness. These remain in the subconscious because we do not recognize the spirit of the person or remember the conflicts with them in the past life. It takes some enlightenment to realize that recurring negative experiences are not random and that there could be a deeper meaning connecting them together.

Often this cycle of conflict plays out within the family. This is the case because conflicted spirits are given opportunities to overcome their differences by being incarnated repeatedly into the same family, often in a role reversal—walking in the shoes of another. For instance, an abusive father becomes the child of the abused son. Does the pattern of abuse continue with the abused son seeking revenge on the abusive father, or can a loving relation develop to overcome the spiritual conflict this time around? Some conflicts can take many lifetimes to be resolved.

We bring much with us into each lifetime, and not all of it is desirable. It is important for the success of our lives to recognize the possibility that the baggage we carry can be from a previous lifetime. Some cultures call this karma or fate. It is our actions and relationships in one lifetime that create the fate we endure in coming incarnations. The sooner we recognize the source of the karma, the quicker we can start working to correct it.

CHAPTER 3

Sins Against the Spirit

NASA has a lot of very smart people, but the questions that come to mind are why are there perhaps two exceptionally creative people—geniuses—among every hundred of us? Is it genetic or is it learned? Nature or nurture? Do you think the 2 percent were born geniuses or worked hard to become the way they are? To answer these questions, Dr. Land administered the test to 1,600 children between the ages of four and five. What he found shocked him: The percentage of children who tested at the genius level of creativity was 98 percent. Can you imagine that? The universal odds of being born a genius are 98 percent!

Dr. Land decided to re-test these children every five years, and again, the results were shocking. By the age of 10, the percentage of those testing at the genius level dropped by 68 points to 30 percent. By the age of 15, it was 12 percent, and for the one million adults tested afterward, it was down to 2 percent.[14]

IN THIS CHAPTER I WILL examine the physical conditions that can injure the spirit in the current lifetime. When a spirit enters its incarnation, it can arrive with the spiritual injuries mentioned in the previous chapter, but it also has inherent talents and gifts. The aforementioned NASA study shows that these diverse gifts are the norm in young children. I have known kindergarten teachers who consider themselves blessed to be taught each

---

[14] Ammar Charani, "Are You a Creative Genius?" *Purposehood: Transform Your Life, Transform the World* (PHD Publishing, 2020), 5–6.

day by a classroom full of these geniuses, but unfortunately that viewpoint is not widely held.

Regrettably, there are countless reasons why the spirit of a child is unable to nurture its spiritual gifts and talents. They are restricted by social norms and parental ego, and in the worst-case, indoctrination, or brainwashing. As a result, their inherent genius is lost, and it is difficult to recover it later in life, if at all.

The societal expectations, depending on where the spirit is incarnated, place various restrictions on the developmental options for the child. School systems are designed to achieve specific outcomes, allowing certain types of talents to flourish while others are downplayed or oppressed or even considered taboo. Sir Ken Robinson's research concludes that we are collectively "Out of Our Minds" in how we teach children today, saying that almost all systems teach children out of their inherent genius by rewarding the wrong behaviors.[15] Schools limit creativity by focusing on academic success and not allowing creativity to develop by accepting failure and using it to build resilience. Many children become risk-averse because the penalty for failure is too high.

Then we have the expectations that parents place on the child, limiting its ability to pursue its spiritual mission in life. People universally agree our future depends on our children. But how this intension is put into practice varies greatly from family to family and often conflicts with the spirit of the child. For some families it means indoctrination into the parental orthodox belief system, which can greatly damage the spirit of an enlightened child. Orthodoxy tolerates no discussion or curiosity or investigation into the truth. It is simply accepted at any cost, and often the payment is free will.

Equally dangerous can be the ego of a parent or the parents. Some want to relive their childhood vicariously through their own child. Some have distinct expectations about their family life and the roles that each person should play in this "ideal" family. Others want to commercialize their children to financially support the family or to fulfill the parent's dream.

---

[15] Ken Robinson, *Out of Our Minds: Learning to Be Creative* (Capstone, 2011).

Few parents are truly able to allow their children enough space to discover their gifts and are also willing to support them unconditionally.

It is the loss of these gifts—or more precisely, a lack of fertile ground for them to grow—that forms the basis for spiritual depression. The spirit becomes frustrated at the restrictions the physical environment presents. Their life circumstances hinder them in pursuing their spiritual purpose, realizing their spiritual life goal, or practicing a rewarding talent. The more obstacles that stand in the way of spiritual fulfillment, the greater the spiritual depression.

Fortunately, some spirits are incarnated into environments that provide a fertile ground for their spiritual genius to thrive. In part two of this book, I will describe how parents can create a supportive environment to preserve and develop the spiritual gifts their children bring into this lifetime. It might mean going against societal norms or family tradition, especially when parents have a child with gifts neither can relate to. This was the case for me. My daughter is gifted in all the areas where I am weak, and she is weak in those areas where I am gifted. It took me some time to acquire the patience required to allow her to take a path unknown to me.

I remember watching the look of dread on her face on the day before the start of the school year when she was twelve. She was gazing at her weekly schedule, and I asked why she was so depressed. She said, "There is not one day of the week I can look forward to." After looking at the schedule, I told her to go back to her desk and write a schedule that she would like. This time when she came back, she had a little smile on her face when she showed me the schedule. After glancing at it, I told her, "This is what your mother would want. Why don't you go back and write down what you truly want?"

This time she came back with a spring in her stride and a gracious smile on her face. She had given up completive swimming and playing the violin, in which she had invested respectively six and four years. These were the two most successful areas of her school life until now. So I asked, why? She said: "I am a successful swimmer, but it is lonely and does not bring me joy." She told me that she had come a long way with the violin, but she could not sing while playing, so she would rather learn to play the piano, and she could do both. She switched from swimming to dance and acting, which started her on a new path with great enthusiasm. The extracurricular enthusiasm carried through to her academic life, giving her positive energy and motivation for academic success.

I pick up this topic again in chapter 10, where I discuss the benefits of letting go of the outcome and focusing on the journey. I wish I had learned this skill at the age of twelve instead of forty-five.

CHAPTER 4

Young Souls

We fallen, have been away from Heaven so long that we need to relearn how to be noble and virtuous. Therefore, the material world was created, to be a place where we are able to have fresh starts, not being burdened with this tragic past in each life until we have advanced enough to confront it. All the while, Lucifer is trying to maintain power over his diminishing kingdom. Trying everything to keep his subjects under his control and keep us from returning home. Like us, he lost his wisdom and reason in the fall, but not his intelligence. Therefore, our task is to relearn the wisdom and reason that we have lost, so that we can recognize the rhetoric that brought us here.[16]

THE FINAL CATEGORY OF SPIRITUAL ailment that I will discuss comes directly from the Fall and the long time our spirit has lived in darkness, lacking wisdom and often reason. The restoration of the fallen is a long, tedious process, covering many lifetimes, as many as thirty. In my work, I have broken this process into three stages starting from selfish (young soul) and progressing to selfless (old soul). The process is slow, and it is not a straight path. There are always chances for setbacks along the path, sometimes setting us back multiple successful lifetimes.

At the beginning of the restoration process, the young soul is a person who is concentrating their efforts on their self. They have few virtues and cannot be expected to display empathy for others. They are often destined for troublesome lifetimes where they can learn patience, compassion, and

---

[16] Shawn T. Murphy, *Torn Between Two Worlds: Material and Ethereal* (CreateSpace Independent Publishing Platform, 2017), 44.

empathy. It is crucial to understand the level of their spiritual development and enlightenment when designing the most supportive environment for these young souls. Ideally, they need good role models and preferably few options, so they do not get into too much trouble.

It can take many lifetimes to overcome the base instincts acquired during the eternity that our spirits spent in the darkness. As I said previously, it can take up to thirty lifetimes to reacquire the virtues that we lost, to gain humility, faith, generosity, compassion, diligence, temperance, and hope. Intelligence is not a virtue and high intelligence without virtue is a dangerous combination. The most recognizable young soul is the narcissist, and they can be dangerous to themselves and their surroundings if they come into money or power.

It is estimated nearly half of those born today are young souls who are here for the first time. Many of these young souls end up dying at a young age, but there is a plan behind this.

> Because this mother's soul knew that this child had died at the age of three and that she had been sad about it and cried for the loss of the child. But now, in the spiritual realm, they gave her the explanation for it.
>
> Back then as a human being it meant her pain and suffering. Now you could give her the explanation: "You see, we took this child that we gave you from below. That was intentional and recorded in his life plan, that it would only have a short time to live, that three years would be enough. The profit—this short life—was of great importance for the little spirit concerned, after all, it came to the children's paradise."
>
> When he was only three years old, this person's mind was not that advanced, so it had not yet grown. According to the spiritual body he had exactly the measure of the earthly body. Because the spiritual body grows with the earthly body. Now this child was welcomed into the children's

paradise, where it was looked after with love and care. Another environment was given to this child so that it could grow up in love. Angels of God took care of it. Because that spirit being or spirit child was burdened in its nature.[17]

Souls who incarnate for the first time have a high risk of making matters worse for themselves, digging yet a deep hole to climb out of. By dying at a young age, they have the advantage of growing up with perfect, spiritual parents, with infinite patience. Even knowing this might be the case, it might not provide any solace to the parents who end up losing a young child. The comfort that they might find is, in the end, this was the best thing for the young soul.

The reincarnation mechanism is enormous, yet great care is taken for each soul being incarnated. It is extremely efficient. If it is seen that a child will only live a few days or months, the soul that will gain the most benefit will be incarnated for this short time, not one with an important mission.

---

[17] "2 Abend," *Meditationswoche 1978* (Pro Beatrice, 2014), 41–42 (translated by Google from the German).

CHAPTER 5

What Is the Game?

So, one of the three came [into the spirit world] when it was time for him. Now only relatives were there for a brief greeting, and everyone went their own way afterwards. So, the returnee was now alone and abandoned. He was astonished at this new world, because everything was new to him, and he couldn't find his way around. Then someone came who seemed to want to greet him politely and told him that he would stand by him and would now assign him a good place in the spirit world. The one who greeted him had given him general information and promised him that he would lead him to a blessed place where he could be especially happy. Since he was completely abandoned and no one greeted him further, he was particularly happy to accept the help of this spirit and let him guide him. And what did this spirit say that guided him? "There couldn't be a more beautiful place for you than that I lead you into the earthly church, where you also went to worship. It's a place of worship, and you know that God looks down with pleasure on this place, was built in his honor. There you shall have your blessed home."

This returnee was completely in agreement with this. He already sensed that things were not going well with him. He had—I may use this expression—a guilty conscience. He found that life went on and that he would be held accountable for his crimes. But then he felt relief because he was received in a loving way. So, he hoped for the best—and if he were taken to church, everything would surely be all right.

Well, this stranger to him took him to church. It seemed so strange to him, however; the church was much bigger, it was so deep. And the stranger led him into the depths of this church. First, he had to familiarize himself with the new environment. He found he could penetrate earthly matter and that he was now in this church, that is, he had been led into the depths of the earth, and his former house of God stood above him.

Of course, he was a bit surprised, but believed this was part of the new order, that everything would look different and that he simply had to adapt to this new environment. For he believed he was in good hands and well managed. This stranger, who led him into the depths where this church stood, politely said goodbye to him and said he should linger here now; he would probably get company soon, he would be in good hands, because here the Church of God would stand above him. And he believed him.

But soon he had to find out that he was actually completely abandoned. He tried to escape but failed. Now he found he was locked in. Here he was in the depths, locked in the earth beneath this church, into which he had entered as a person to pray. His spiritual eye could now observe how the believers were walking above his head. Over time, of course, he realized something was wrong, that he had been locked up. He couldn't escape upwards. He watched these people walking above himself but could not get out of his surroundings. Whenever there was a service and the believers were in the church, pacing back and forth above his head, he began to shout. But all shouting was of no use and did not help him. It was so strange for him: They moved around above his head, and yet they did not fall into that depth. He also attempted to pierce the matter with his hands. He could pierce the earth with his hands, but he found himself so heavy that he could not move. (Lene)[18]

HOW CAN YOU PLAY THE game, if you do not know the rules or the players? The afterlife greeting described here illustrates that point. First of all, when this person was alive, he did not believe in the afterlife. So, when he awoke in the spirit world after his physical death, he knew nothing—neither the players nor the rules. He did not understand the only spirit interested in greeting him was the evil spirit who spurred him on during his lifetime. He was ever-present during his human lifetime, encouraging him to fight with his fellow man, keeping the conflict alive with his neighbors. Since this human had followed the wishes of the evil spirit in life, he now became subjected to the will of the same evil spirit in death. Eventually this evil spirit gathered all three of his victims under this church so that the conflict between the three could live on in the afterlife. This evil spirit was able to hold his "devoted friends" captive because they had given in to his will during their human lifetimes. As long as they kept fighting with each other, they would remain under his will. The first rule is:

> *Commitment to evil requires a change of behavior to overcome.*

Here we have an unenlightened spirit entering the afterlife, recognizing that no one took interest in him, except one spirit. He did not question this evil spirit, since he was simply happy to have attention and praise. This is exactly how it works during a human lifetime, except we cannot observe all the spiritual players on the gameboard, and most don't know the rules of the game.

First, the ethereal world is more diverse than the material universe we live in. The population of the ethereal world is vast, so making generalizations about it is unwise. It was one third of the stars of Heaven that were cast into Hell (see Revelation 12:4–9) This is a number in the billions of trillions!

---

[18] Lene, "Vom Wirken der Streiter Michaels," *Meditationswoche 1971*, by Beatrice Brunner (GL Zürich, 2013), 122–124 (Translated from the German by Google).

The Bible refers to these as the waters God needed to separate and place a barrier between them (Genesis 1:6–8) The ancient Greeks referred to this mass of beings as seas, or specifically, the bitter sea (of fallen angels). They called the ruler of the bitter sea Poseidon.

There is much symbolism in this figure created by the enlightened Greek artists, including the fish at his feet and the trident in his hand. The fish reminds us of Jonah and his escape from the bitter sea. The trident symbolizes the three fallen archangels of Heaven that ruled humanity and the underworld in ancient times.[19]

Since the Fall of Heaven, there have been many like Jonah who have escaped the depths of Hell and have either returned to Heaven or are currently on a path of restoration. This means there is a broad spectrum of spiritual beings, from the depths of Hell to the heights of Heaven, and this is what makes our interactions with the spiritual so troublesome. We must find a

---

[19] See Appendix 5: We all have the same spiritual ancestry.

way to discern which ones are active in our human lives, and this is not a simple task. We have enough difficulty recognizing the motives of fellow humans, where we can use all our senses to observe their behavior, judging their action and words. How can we discover the underlying motives of a spirit without seeing or hearing them, merely using a Ouija board? The answer is, we cannot learn anything about the motives of a spirit through a single "reading" or use of a spirit board. It requires many encounters and much experience to trust the motives of the surrounding spirits. This brings us to the second rule:

Test the spirits to discover their motives.

Ghosts are the spirits of materialistic people who have no thoughts of the afterlife, and thus are referred to as lost spirits. When they die, they are not expecting an afterlife, so they often do not realize they are dead. In spirit, they look the same as they did when they were alive as humans. Such spirits continue living their lives, and it may take a long time before they realize they are dead. I had one such ghost living in my house. She kept saying: "You don't belong here; you have to leave before my family comes home." She did not accept that she had died twenty years before and that her family had moved out afterwards. She was still waiting for them to come back home after twenty years.

Dr. Carl Wickland spent thirty years working with ghosts. He accomplished his work because his wife was a talented medium. Even through all the discussions he had with these beings, he never gained any insights into Heaven, Hell, or reincarnation. These lost spirits had no more knowledge after they died than they did while they were living. They carried their beliefs and vices with them into the afterlife, leading us to the third rule:

There is no instant enlightenment after death; the spirit lives on with its virtue and vice.

Ghosts are so unenlightened that they often cannot observe the higher beings around them. Only if the higher beings want to be recognized will they make themselves visible to them. This is a fourth rule:

Enlightenment determines spiritual perspective; a spirit can only perceive at or below their own level.

Each and every person has a guardian spirit assigned to them, whether we believe it or not. It is their responsibility to ensure the spiritual laws are enforced, specifically that evil spirits do not overstep the bounds placed on them.[20] People with good intensions, who are helping others, are assigned additional spiritual specialists to assist their noble works. Dedicated healthcare professionals receive much help in their daily tasks of caring for others, for example. Those people assigned with special tasks in life are given spiritual teachers to prepare them for the hard work ahead of them. With the billions of people living in this world, there are multiples of that number in the ethereal world working either to help or to hinder them. From this, we find two more rules:

Each person has at least one guardian spirit.

Like attracts like; guardians assist those with noble intentions and evil spirits cheer for those loyal to them.

In Dr. Fiore's work,[21] she treated a patient who was possessed by the spirit of her dead sister. The spirit gained access because the surviving sister pledged to do anything to help her dying sibling. Through this, the spirit of the dead sister received permission to use her sister's physical body. This example is an unintended consequence of the following rule:

Free will takes the highest priority.

The divine spirits cannot act against your free will, but they do have methods help their charges to see reason. Possessing spirits can be thought of as vampires, and they can be defended against in the same mythical ways known in pop culture. Like a vampire, a spirit of any kind cannot enter your home (your spiritual self) without being invited. The evil spirits can be repelled with your belief, not simply a physical symbol, but with true faith.

---

[20] See Appendix 1: Final Judgment.
[21] Fiore, *The Unquiet Dead.*

In addition, these vampires can be expelled by rescinding permission and taking your power back with your free will, discussed in chapter 11.

There are many more lost spirits than only those actively molesting humans, as I have discovered in my research and from close friends. One such friend is named Elizabeth, whom I have known for over twenty-five years. I have followed the development of her spiritual gifts, which she has pursued in a systematic and scientific fashion. She has been using these enhanced gifts to heal people in her local village and others around the world. She has also passed on the experience she gained to her students, empowering other healers to be more effective in their own healing methods and in their prayers.

Elizabeth was sent a child teacher to develop her skills in clairvoyance and spiritual healing. Working together with a clairvoyant prepubescent youth allowed Elizabeth[22] to conduct countless experiments in prayers, hands-on healing, and distant healing, receiving third-party verification of her spiritual impact. Over time, this youth helped Elizabeth to develop her own clairvoyance.

Clairvoyance is skill like many others. With much practice, many can learn to play the piano, for example, but few have the talent to become a virtuoso. Besides the skill aspect of clairvoyance, there is another limiting factor— one's own spiritual maturity. A skilled clairvoyant still cannot see further than their own enlightenment will allow.

> *Clairvoyance is a rare skill that requires proficiency, and it is limited by virtue.*

The good news is that we also have many allies in the ethereal world, not solely foes. Remember, only one third of Heaven fell; two-thirds are there waiting for us. Not only are they waiting, but they are actively helping us to return. It is the spirits of dead family members that might haunt us during our lives, but not the spiritual family members that we left behind. They are

---

[22] Elisabeth Vonderau, *Begegnungen Mit Verstorbenen Erlebnisberichte*, (August Von Goethe Literaturverlag, 2017)

cheering us on and helping us be spiritually successful in our time on earth. The allies do not stop there. Other sentient beings in the ethereal world also help us through our daily lives, as I describe in chapter 7.

Finally, what are the stakes of the game? I describe Will's personal battle in chapter 11, but here he describes the battle lost by his dear friend Kimberley. This is what is at stake.

(Will) "I believe God brought us together. We met at Celebrate Recovery. It is a Christian Recovery group. Right away, we realized we had a lot in common. Especially, what the dark spirits have done to us. Lies made up in order to ruin our lives. They were able to slander us in similar ways. A method used by these spirits on several people I have come across on my journey. Terrible lies about good people. We bonded right away. We were both looking for answers, church, recovery, psychiatry, etc. We got support from each.

"Right away, I had seen she was in the very early stages of harassment. She didn't understand what or why this was happening. She was very confused, trying her best to live a normal life under very surreal and quite unfair circumstances. She gravitated towards psychiatry and mental illness as an explanation of what she was experiencing.

"She had a 7-year-old son. His father wasn't in the picture and I am happy the good Lord decided not to bless me with children or a family for that matter. We bonded right away. We used to play catch, soccer, talked about life. He had it. Whatever it is. He knew things that no one could possibly know.

"After witnessing one of her attacks, I knew that demonic forces were at work. She told me she swore that I was plotting against her with other people. Things were appearing and disappearing. She was angry and frustrated. One day she confided to me that she was thinking about ending it. I had seen how much she was suffering. They were doing to her the same thing they did to me. I thought she could take it. Plus, she had a son who loved and adored her. She wouldn't actually do it. I said the same thing myself all the time.

"We worked together. One morning on our way to work. I noticed that she was perceiving everything I was saying wrong. No matter what I said she would misinterpret it or flat out misunderstand. Our language was confused, and we couldn't communicate. We didn't speak after that. Someone or something didn't want us talking anymore. Sadly, a month or two later I was informed by a member of the church we went to that she ended her life. Her son was orphaned.

"It is in this writer's opinion that she was murdered by a network of nefarious spirits. Driven to suicide. It happens every day.

"These spirits target people and will not stop until they are destroyed. This is why this work is so important. Sadly, the mainstream refuses to except the TRUTH. Her death will go down as another suicide due to mental health issues. However, the truth is much more disturbing."

Suicide is the loss of a spiritual battle

Each incarnation as a human is accompanied by a life-plan which has tests and objectives for the lifetime. If the evil spiritual world can convince a person to willfully abandon their life-plan, they can claim victory. The loser will have to start over - this is the cost of losing a spiritual battle.

CHAPTER 6

Summary of Part One

I would now like to explain something about the gnomes who live near humans. This gnome-clan, as I would like to call them, are on the one hand helpful, conversely they are very quarrelsome among their siblings. These gnomes also put themselves in the service of humans, and you will hear why later. First, I would like to talk about where these gnomes live. They can be found in the woods, in the barns and stables, in any house, which means that maybe that's saying too much. They go to those houses where people live whom they like. They never stay where people live who they dislike—that happens too. So, they are in the woods, they are with the animals in the stables, they are in the open field, they are in the mountains, they are in the water, in the gardens, in the bushes. They also have their shelter which they build themselves according to the tastes they own. Some are demanding, others undemanding. (Lene)[23]

IN THE FIRST PART OF this book, I have explained the various types of spiritual ailments that one can be born with and one can acquire during life. I have provided references for further explanations of each, as it is not the purpose of this book to prove each of the concepts presented here. The purpose is to be thorough enough, so it is possible for the reader to recognize a potential spiritual cause of a physical symptom. So, when the traditional treatments are not working, there is still hope for an effective spiritual treatment plan. The references provided should allow the reader to research in more depth potential spiritual ailments that could be at play.

---

[23] "Die Welt der Gnomen, Elfen und Feen", *Geistige Welt* 2018, no. 1: 4 (Translated from the German by Google).

The accuracy of the diagnosis is not as critical as you might expect. The treatments that are recommended in the second part of the book are nonaddictive methodologies that can be used alongside any medications your doctor may have prescribed. They can also be used effectively in combination. This will be critical in cases like the one described at the end of chapter 1, where the subject is being influenced by multiple entities, each with their own motivations.

As described in that case, we appreciate how multiple spiritual influences and ailments can exist simultaneously. This person is possessed by the spirit of a deceased man, under the control of the will of a human and an evil spirit. This example also demonstrates how foreign spirits gain access to us—either at times of weakness or through our own will. Giving your will up to another person or spirit is easy to do when you ask to be put under hypnosis, for example. Furthermore, we are most often physically weak when we are in the hospital, and this is a place full of spirits who can take advantage of our spiritual and physical weakness.

The first part to this book is written to help you recognize the signs that may indicate a spiritual cause of a physical ailment. Being able to acknowledge a problem is the first step to curing it. There are many ailments that I have discussed, not limited to a young soul, where the person in question is not capable of the self-awareness required to recognize their ailment. These are the people who could benefit the most by a successful treatment of their spiritual ailment. But it is too much to expect that they seek help themselves. In the second part of the book, I recommend strategies to assist in these cases, and how those around can help without being drawn in. In addition, we will discover the many other types of spiritual beings who reside in the ethereal world and are willing to help if we ask, like the quarrelsome gnomes. A smile always comes across my face when I think of how these sentient and talented folk are able to assist humans so well. They do it by not taking us, and themselves so seriously.

CHAPTER 7

Introduction to Healing

Aura of an enlightened person

The aura has almost reached the shape of the circle. The properties are balanced, their colors have been arranged harmoniously. The radiation around the figure forms the shape of the ankh, the Egyptian handle cross, the symbol for the developed "third eye." In the aura of an enlightened one, the properties are only expressed in radiation, no longer in forms. The developing human has to live through the lower qualities in many incarnations in order to be able to overcome them. The enlightened one is not without these qualities, but he has overcome them—that is, transformed [them] into positive ones—within himself.

Thrift, for example, and the gathering and stocking up of supplies is inherently natural, combined with self-addiction it results in greed. If the ego-addiction disappears, then frugality remains. The advanced is sparing with himself, but gives his possessions for others with joy. The higher insight prevents him from helping in the wrong place, where it does more harm than good. With his gifts he alleviates real misery in a needy [one] or creates joy and strength for a friend or companion with them. Just as with thrift and avarice it is with the positive and negative aspects of all other qualities.

The greatest outward virtue of an enlightened person is his simplicity, modesty, and humility. Through his selfless love and the light of God shining through him, he is a kind, all-understanding friend and brother, a mediator between the realms of light and the hardships of the earth for all beings who meet him.[24]

I START THE SECOND HALF of the book with an inspirational goal for the spiritual healing process. Every human being can aspire to this full potential, and therefore, all the suggestions from this book can be used to move closer to this goal, regardless of the current state of spiritual health you find yourself in. In this part of the book are found the various tools available to overcome the spiritual afflictions that you or your loved ones may suffer from. At the end of this book, you should not only have tools to assist you but also have a guide as to how they can be implemented in your life.

[24] Weigl and Wenzel, *Die entschleierte Aura*, 39, 108.

Comparing the image in chapter 1 to this image, the abundance of light colors stands out, reflecting the high level of enlightenment of the spiritual person depicted here. This is a goal that everyone can strive for: the stronger and brighter we are spiritually, the more capacity we have to protect and heal ourselves and our family and to help others.

There are many sources of positive spiritual energy in the world, in the surrounding nature: the mountain streams, the oceans, the sunlight, and the flowers, to name a few. Those who have access to the forest, mountains, streams, and oceans can benefit from these natural healing energies. For those who live in the city, there are also ways to replicate these natural energies and bring them into your city life. Two of the most well recognized experts in these fields are Dr. Edward Bach[25] (flowers) and Dr. Masaru Emoto[26] (water). Dr. Emoto has studied this problem in Japan and developed techniques for those living the city, away from nature.

The Bach flower remedies are sold worldwide, and they contain the spiritual essence of various flowers at the peak of their bloom. The flowers are picked on a sunny day and placed in water, allowing the energy from the sun to carry the spiritual essence of the flower into the water. Drops from these thirty-eight different waters are used to treat many spiritual illnesses including fear, anxiety, obsessiveness, hopelessness, and despair. The beauty of the flower remedies is they can be used in conjunction with other medications without the fear of any interaction, as they are not chemically based. The energy they carry is what is called *odic force*, the same energy as seen in the aura at the beginning of this chapter. Therefore, they are perfect for self-diagnosis and can be self-administered.

The groundbreaking work by Masaru Emoto has opened the minds of many to the power of thought through his experiments with water crystals. He examined the formation of water crystals from water exposed to various conditions, including all types of music and a range of thoughts. He found the crystals formed under positive thought-energy were perfect while those

---

[25] F. J. Wheeler, *Bach Flower Remedies* (Keats Pub Inc, 1998).
[26] Masaru Emoto, *The True Power of Water: Healing and Discovering Ourselves* (Pocket, 2005).

formed under negative thought-energy were malformed. The experiments have been repeated, demonstrating that thought or, more precisely, intent has a powerful spiritual influence on water.

The connection between these water experiments and the human body is obvious, since the human body is mostly water. We can imagine how are our children, for example, are affected by the negative or the positive thoughts that we project to them. Clairvoyants, who can see into the spiritual realm, have confirmed the buildup of dark energy around a person who is the target of negative thoughts, to the point that all this dark odic energy forms a demon, as was discussed in chapter 1.

The good news is that positive thoughts can overcome negative ones, in the same way that the sun eliminates the darkness. Masaru Emoto developed a practice to accomplish this called HADO—*Healing and Discovering Ourselves*. Through this practice, we can enhance the water that we drink with spiritual energy that strengthens and heals us by removing the negative energy we accumulate. This water could also be combined with Bach flower remedies, for example, as the effects are additive.

The less well recognized sources of spiritual energy in nature are in crystals, in spiritual beings that inhabit nature, and in natural spiritual springs around the world. Crystals are another tool that we can use in healing, as each variety provides its own distinct spiritual characteristics.

As early as the 4th millennium BC, the Sumerians named minerals as "miracle stones" in their records. The subtle effects of gemstones were already known to people at that time. The use as jewelry, healing stones, lucky charms or grave goods can be proven over thousands of years and on the most varied of continents. All known high cultures revered them for their beauty, their protection and their effect on body and soul.

In ancient Egypt they were indispensable for rulers and priests, at whose death they were taken to the grave. Kings of all cultures and continents have always felt connected to precious stones, as the rich treasures from ancient times prove. Their crowns were richly adorned with emeralds, diamonds, sapphires and similar treasures.

The natives of America have preserved and passed on their belief in the healing power of gemstones to this day. Well-founded knowledge about that topic comes from this high-quality culture. The Indians have always carried their stones with them in medicine bags, made jewelry from them and meditated with them. They are convinced the crystal carries the primal energy, the life force, and that all conscious life arises from it.

References to the miraculous powers of stones can also be found in the Old Testament. Churches were always adorned and magnificently adorned with them. With the beginning of science and technical progress of our epoch, the knowledge about the healing power was practically lost. What is not visible or rationally comprehensible is not considered true. The gap that this denial of a primal energy, a rootedness in the universe leaves behind in humans, is shown, for example, by the large number of mental illnesses or the high suicide rates around the world.

We have to find a faith again, to feel the eternity of life in us. As a helper on this path, nature with all its treasures is available to us. Whether you want to call the increasing change in consciousness of people in the present time esoteric or whatever name you put this movement under— every expansion of the understanding of the cosmic context has a harmonizing effect.[27],[28]

Selecting the most beneficial crystal can be done intuitively or intellectually with the help of the descriptions of the properties. It is important to care for your crystals over time. It is not uncommon for them to crack when too much energy is drained. Don't panic, though; that means it was energy that you needed. To avoid this, they should be regularly recharged in a mountain stream, the open ocean, or the sunshine. But you should replace those that do crack.

---

[27] Verena Nowak, *Universum der Edelsteine* (VN-Verl., 1994), 7 (Translated from the German by Google).
[28] Grove and Grotto, "Gemstones and Their Meanings" (flyer), www.groveandgrotto. com/products/gemstones-and-their-meanings-flyer?variant=12795383447665.

Often known only to children, the wee spiritual beings that live in the gardens, parks, and forests can be an additional source of healing and protection. They often bring comfort to children but can also help adults. It only takes a belief in the elves, fairies, and gnomes to get them to help you during your time of need.[29] Gnomes are very loyal, if you can convince them to help. But they can be cantankerous as described at the beginning of chapter 6. Please do not discourage your child's *imaginary friends* as their presence in our lives is beneficial for all, and should not be made to feel unwelcome in your home.

---

[29] Flower A. Newhouse, *Die Engel der Natur* (Aquamatin Verlag, 1996), 38.

CHAPTER 8

Modes of Healing

Man can use also the od of plants, beasts and minerals as remedies for his own ailments. It is upon this reciprocal transfer of od that the laws of healing within God's creation are based. Thus, many living animals radiate a definite od which has healing powers. Those of many plants are widely known, although unfortunately the people of today are not as familiar with the curative properties of certain plants in the case of various diseases as were the ancients. The same is true of the minerals. Most people think it superstition to believe that every precious stone has an odic power of its own, and yet it is precisely the od of precious stones which possesses unusual purity and strength, and invigorates the persons wearing them. It is, of course, essential for the wearer to select the stone best suited to his personal od and possessed of no odic forces which would conflict with the odic radiations of the individual. You have books which will instruct you further as to the right precious stones, the kind of which is determined by the date of their wearer's birth.

A very important factor in all healing is the transmission of od by one person to another. A sick child feels better immediately when its mother snuggles it against her body, for by so doing she transmits her own healthy od to the sick child and strengthens the latter's od which has become enfeebled by sickness. A healthy person who sleeps with sick or old people imparts a share of his odic force to them. His sick or old bed-fellows are invigorated thereby while the healthy person grows steadily weaker by the continued expenditure of his od. That is the reason why healthy persons who sleep with old or sick people for any great length of time take on a sickly appearance, which is a consequence of the loss of their odic force, and for the same reason children should not be allowed to sleep in the same bed with old folks.[30]

JOHANNES GREBER EXPLAINS THE INTUITION of the child to seek healing energy from its mother, and there is much available. There is healing energy throughout nature that has served humanity well, for those who have been able to recognize this resource. There have been experts in many narrow fields in the past, but fortunately for us today, we have access to the spectrum of these inspirational works to draw from. We will break down the major ways in which these energies can be used. How we utilize these energies in our daily lives requires creating new habits and practicing them. Again, we can call on proven methods of implementing energy work in our routines.

Attitude

Our attitude toward life plays a major part in our health, specifically through happiness and its impact on mental and physical health. We can maintain a positive attitude by the perspective that we choose—is the glass half empty, or is it half full? To rephrase this, are we grateful for the water in the glass, or are we jealous or angry about the missing half? Being grateful for the things

---

[30] Johannes Greber, "The Law of Vital, or Odic Force," *Communication with the Spirit World of God: Its Laws and Purpose: Extraordinary Experiences of a Catholic Priest* (6th ed.) (Johannes Greber Memorial Foundation, 1979), 78–79.

you have brings your life into harmony in the same way it brings water into harmony as shown in the research from Dr. Emoto.[31]

The power of positive thinking is factual, but achieving it is tangible work. This is why Byron Katie[32] calls it simply "The Work." She has dedicated her life to helping people achieve joy in their lives through this very important practice, and you can start this practice today for free on her website, thework. com. Positivity and gratitude in your prayers are just as important: when you give, you receive multiples in return, so give gratitude and happiness.

Atmosphere

We have control over the atmosphere within which we live our lives, regardless of our income. The music we play, the plants and the art we decorate our living space with can all give us energy or drain us – we have to choose. The Chinese practice of *feng shui* is a good place to start.

Nutrition

What you use to nourish your body has an impact on your spirit as well. In addition to eating as low on the food chain as possible, it is important to consider where the food has originated, including who has harvested and prepared it. For instance, Sikhs are spiritual people, and some Sikhs will only eat food prepared by their own families. The reasoning behind this is simple: they know the quality of the odic force of the person preparing their food. The people who grew, harvested, and prepared the food have left their spiritual imprint on the food, including their emotions.

Gratitude is a tool that can be used in all aspects of your life. For example, the expression of true gratefulness for the food on the table, those who prepared it, and those who grew it can turn mere nourishment into true spiritual nourishment for you and all those in the supply chain.

---

[31] Emoto, *True Power of Water*, 58.
[32] Byron Katie, *A Thousand Names for Joy: Living in Harmony With the Way Things Are* (Three Rivers Press, 2008).

Working with Nature and the Cosmos

Both cosmic healing energies and earthly healing energies have been discovered, and some are well known. Blanche Merz is a spiritual researcher who has documented many of these places around the world, and I refer you to her work to find locations near you.

In our modern world, many have overlooked the natural rhythms of the earth and the cosmos. We expend energy when we work against these natural rhythms and gain it when working in harmony. One example is eating local foods when they are in season instead of maintaining the same diet year-round. This is recommended by numerous holistic nutritionists, as in Ayurveda.[33] Fighting against the forces the moon exerts on nature is equally as wasteful, and working with the moon can be beneficial.

> **The Misunderstood Moon** – Today we have only a feeble knowledge in the field of cosmo-telluric influences; in any event we must not forget to mention the Moon.
>
> Our ancestors knew more about it than we do. Even if we have now set foot on the Moon, they had a real knowledge that we have too often sought to ridicule. Inasmuch as this learning was only transmitted orally, many useful aspects risk being lost with the disappearance of our grandfathers. And, nevertheless, in observing out of curiosity or in testing these stated rules we can only remain perplexed before the results, and finally we must bow before the facts.
>
> During the five nights of full moon—the three which precede the full clarity of the moon and the two which follow—the terrestrial magnetic field is modified and has a certain influence on these "lunatic" human beings, on sleep, on births. Studies of the subject have demonstrated that the wave length of cosmic waves having a normal length of 21 centimetres (8 inches) is reduced by 50 per

---

[33] https://www.hopkinsmedicine.org/health/wellness-and-prevention/ayurveda.

cent, down to 10.5 centimetres (4 inches). Modification of the oscillating circuit thus perturbs the oscillatory equilibrium of the human cell; remember that the healthy cell has a frequency of 27 megahertz (one MHz = one million vibrations per second).

What must we think, when our elders never grafted a tree during a waning moon; otherwise the tree would no longer bear fruit during a fixed number of years. Yet our present-day biological farmers apply these natural rules more and more. They plant what must bear fruit and leaves during a period of waxing moon, and they plant vegetables which must develop below ground during the waning moon.

Within the rhythm of our actions in relation to the moon everything that must be consolidated, constructed or augmented will succeed when the operations begin during a period of increasing moon and when the illuminated part of the moon is at the right (and movements toward the right will be favoured).

In contrast, everything that must be eliminated, purified or extracted will be facilitated during a period of decreasing moon, with the illuminated part of the moon at the left (and movements toward the left will be favoured). Let he who has never heard this mentioned before shake his head, but he who wants to try the experiment will be astonished and rewarded.

The moon is the life rhythm star par excellence.[34]

Further away, the cosmic forces also impact our lives in a rhythmic manner. Therefore, it is important when you were born and understand your personal rhythm within the cosmos—when you are working with the forces of the cosmos and when you are working against them.

---

[34] Blanche Merz, *Points of Cosmic Energy* (CW Daniel Co. Ltd., 1987), 150–151.

Cleaning House

I would suggest making a ritual out of cleaning the house and doing it on a regular basis with mindfulness. Take the opportunity of clear, sunny days to air out your apartment or house. Visualize the clean air and sunshine dissolving all the negativity in your home, replacing it with fresh air and optimism. Together with gratitude, you can add incense or burning sage to your ritual. Don't be shy in asking your family members to participate in this ritual, and you can even invite your guardian angel(s) to do their part in cleaning the home spiritually. Use a large glass bowl filled with clean water to capture the negative spiritual energy while cleaning your house. Discard the water carefully when the process is completed.

Life-Long Commitment of en*Light*enment

The best way to maintain health and to fight off the negativity that can be part of life is with light, and this is one of the many meanings of enlightenment. The goal of the second part of this book was clear, as given in the opening image of the enlightened soul. Enlightenment is a continuum, so one does not become enlightened; rather, becomes more enlightened, and there is no upper limit.

This process is twofold; it is not only through meditation and pleasant thoughts, but it must also be accompanied by noble actions and education. Love and knowledge are the keys to enlightenment. It can be supported by a ritual of daily reflection at the end of the day, to take inventory of the activities that cost energy and those that provided energy. It is important to be grateful and forgiving, especially to yourself.

Pain and Tears

It was only during my review of the final edits to this book I realized I had avoided an important concept. As I started the hike with my family this morning, I noticed the pain in my left knee, left hip, left elbow and left shoulder. This pain on my left side had been growing for the past six months, and I mentioned it for the first time to my daughter. She said she had been thinking about the discussions we recently had with a close friend about pain. I was reminded of this discussion, and during the rest of the hike, this chapter ending developed.

As I demonstrated, humans tend to avoid pain at all costs, often to their own detriment. This is signified today by the opioid crisis and a general tendency to reach for pain relief of any kind, before confronting it. The pain may be caused from injury, loss, shame, disappointment, rejection, or other sources, including spiritual ones.

Going through the pain is actually part of the healing process. In his work, Jim Warner[35] describes the importance of going through the pain to achieve authenticity and joy in your life. By accepting that pain is an important part of life, we open our lives up to the opportunity of achieving pure joy - without pain there is no joy.

Pain is both a mode of healing and an important diagnostic tool. Pain is part of the spiritual healing process, it is necessary in the pursuit of virtue, and therefore something to be thankful for. Without it, life on Earth would be meaningless. So, be thankful for the message that your body or spirit is sending to you, and be curious about the message it wants to portray: does it want you to call the doctor or your estranged parent?

There are three sources of uncontrollable tears: 1) from physical pain 2) from emotional pain, and 3) from spiritual pain. With the latter being the most uncontrollable. When I have any type of spiritual experience, I cry. It took me many years to find out why I only cry, and not laugh. I came to the conclusion that they are both tears of joy and pain my soul is expressing. Crying is the most effective communication method my soul has to reach my intellect.

Only when I asked myself the question, "Why do I have this pain on my left side?" did the thought process engage. By the end of our hike, the

---

[35] Jim Warner, *Facing Pain - Embracing Love*, (OnCourse Publishing, 2012)

pains in my left side had retreated, and I thanked my guardian for his efforts in bringing this subject to the surface. In the next chapter, I discuss the topic of meditation, and the root cause of pain is always a fruitful topic to meditate on.

CHAPTER 9

Meditation

We also have our spiritual bread, our spiritual wine, our foods and so many wonderful fruits—not only you. You should not think, however, that we consume these things in the same way as you, who must eat because you are hungry. We do not feel hunger, but we enjoy these wonderful fruits and have delight and joy in them. We consume them in a different way. From these spiritual fruits we have a very pure power at our disposal for human beings. We can offer such fruits to a human being so that they barely sense it, or perhaps not at all. A human who is well protected by an angelic being can be brought such food and drink regularly throughout the day. We also have our medicines, which we bring to human beings. We spirits of God do not need these medicines—we only have them for human beings. We take this spiritually-pure power from our gardens, from these meadows, from the ponds, from the spiritual flowers, from their roots and so on—the purest power, the purest form—and offer it to human beings. (Lene)[36]

THE MOST EFFECTIVE SPIRITUAL HEALING is a result of forming a relationship with your friends in the spiritual world. When you build up a true friendship with your guardian spirit and long-lost friends, there is much that they can do, as Lene just described. The best-known reference to this phenomenon is the manna that sustained Moses and the Israelites in the desert. This "manna" is the spiritual bread Lene speaks of that can sustain human life. It is the same nourishment that Jesus received during

---

[36] "Heavenly Sources of Healing for Body and Soul," *The Spiritual World*, vol. 2020, no. 4: 3–8.

His long retreats into the desert where His physical body was fully sustained from spiritual food. This is the unseen nourishment your guardians bring you when you are following your path and are in need of it.

An intimate relationship with your spirit guide is an extraordinary accomplishment to achieve, and it can be a lengthy journey to achieve this, but you should not be discouraged by that. Each step on this journey adds significant value to both your physiology and to your spiritual health.

A first major step is mindfulness, becoming mindful of your own being. For this step, Bob Hoffman developed the Quadrinity model[37] of the human being. It goes beyond the mind-body-soul model that some use to describe our essence. It splits the mind into two separate entities: intellect and emotion. I find this perceptive from Hoffman, considering he created this model long before the medical community discovered the crucial importance of the "second brain" located in the gut, which is separate from the intellect. The following article from *Scientific American* summarizes the importance of the "second brain."

> A deeper understanding of this mass of neural tissue, filled with important neurotransmitters, is revealing it does much more than merely handle digestion or inflict the occasional nervous pang. The little brain in our innards, in connection with the big one in our skulls, partly determines our mental state and plays key roles in certain diseases throughout the body ….
>
> "The system is way too complicated to have evolved only to make sure things move out of your colon," says Emeran Mayer, professor of physiology, psychiatry and biobehavioral sciences at the David Geffen School of Medicine at the University of California, Los Angeles (U.C.L.A.). For example, scientists were shocked to learn

---

[37] Tim Laurence, *The Hoffman Process: The World-Famous Technique That Empowers You to Forgive Your Past, Heal Your Present, and Transform Your Future* (Bantam Books, 2004).

that about 90 percent of the fibers in the primary visceral nerve, the vagus, carry information from the gut to the brain and not the other way around. "Some of that info is decidedly unpleasant," Gershon says.

The second brain informs our state of mind in other more obscure ways, as well. "A big part of our emotions are probably influenced by the nerves in our gut," Mayer says. Butterflies in the stomach—signaling in the gut as part of our physiological stress response, Gershon says—is but one example. Although gastrointestinal (GI) turmoil can sour one's moods, everyday emotional well-being may rely on messages from the brain below to the brain above. For example, electrical stimulation of the vagus nerve—a useful treatment for depression—may mimic these signals, Gershon says ....

Down the road, the blossoming field of neurogastroenterology will likely offer some new insight into the workings of the second brain—and its impact on the body and mind. "We have never systematically looked at [the enteric nervous system] in relating lesions in it to diseases like they have for the" central nervous system, Gershon says. One day, perhaps there will be well-known connections between diseases and lesions in the gut's nervous system as some in the brain and spinal cord today indicate multiple sclerosis.[38]

When using mindfulness techniques, we should acknowledge all aspects of our physique—intellect, emotional self, and our body. The body has much to tell us, if we listen closely. Unfortunately, many shield themselves from the messages the body is communicating to us due to a dominant intellect—mind over matter. By finding balance between the intellect, the emotional self, and the body, we allow more information to be processed

---

[38] Adam Hadhazy, "Think Twice: How the Gut's 'Second Brain' Influences Mood and Well-Being," *Scientific American*, 12 Feb. 2010, www.scientificamerican.com/article/gut-second-brain/.

about our well-being. Achieving this balance is the first goal on our path to spiritual enlightenment.

The second level of mindfulness is becoming mindful of your shadows and your inner child. This is where my personal journey began: the search to rediscover my inner child. It was not until I was forty-five that I realized what I had lost in my childhood—the wide-eyed curiosity and creativity that I once possessed. It was witnessing this in my own child that awakened the longing to search for what I had lost.

Another important step is meditation, and again, there are two levels of meditation. The one most widely touted today is a physiological goal—to reduce stress and extend healthy life. This is accomplished through meditation of movement—movement of energy within the body. It can be done through simple deep-breathing exercises, which activate the parasympathetic nervous system, allowing free flowing of energy throughout the body. Many cultures have this type of meditation in their ancient practices.

For instance, *qi gong* and tai chi have many movements helpful for energy balancing and for stimulating the vagus nerve and the parasympathetic nervous system. Here are four beneficial movement types for this purpose.

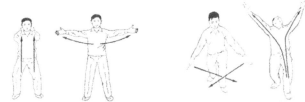

(1) Open Expand Your Chest   (2) Grabbing the Sea to Look Up at the Sky

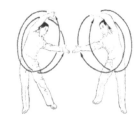

(3) Flying Like an Eagle   (4) Circling Your Body Like a Windmill
(left and right)

Directions:

- Coordinate movements of arms with deep breathing.
- Be mindful of your breath, inhale positive energy and exhale negative thoughts.
- When breathing, the stomach expands during inhaling and contracts during exhaling. This is deep breathing.
- When arms are raised, inhale. When arms are lowered, exhale.
- When arms close, inhale. When the arms open, exhale.
- When palm or fist pulls in, inhale. When palm or fist pushes out, exhale.
- When your arms lower, bend your knees and sink into the floor with the focus of weight in the "bubbling well" of your feet (on ball of foot between big and second toes).

In yoga, the sun salutation ritual lends itself well for the physiological purpose and has the added benefit of containing the spiritual symbolism of the cycle of life and renewal. Here is a guide to this meditation.

1. Begin standing in the *Mountain Pose*, hands in the prayer position. Take a moment or two to ground your feet, still your eyes and connect with your breath.

2. Inhale and sweep the arms up above your head to the *Upward Hand Pose*. Reach through the fingertips, and lengthen the sides of the waist.

3. Exhale, draw the belly back and your thigh muscles upwards, soften your knees slightly and fold forward into *Standing Forward Fold* or into a *Half Forward Bend*.

   (Optional) On your exhale, tuck your toes, and send your hips up and back into Downward Facing Dog. Send your chest towards your thighs and lengthen through your arms and shoulders, staying grounding in your hands with finger spread. Engage your core and thighs. Press your heels towards the ground as much as you can.

4. On your inhale, lift your head up to look forward. Bend the knees and step the right leg back into a *High Lunge*. Firm the top of the right thigh up, draw the left hip slightly back and keep the spine long.

5. Hold the breath in, plant the palms and step the left leg back to join the right in the *Plank*. Press strongly into the hands, firm the front of the body into the back of the body, and keep the neck in line with the spine.

6. Inhale and roll forward and upwards into *Upward Facing Dog*. Press the hands into the floor, shine your heart up and out, and roll the shoulders down the back.

7. On your inhale, slide your entire body onto the ground, untucking your toes, and lift up through your chest, straightening your arms, coming into *Cobra*. In full cobra your head, chest, and abdomen are lifted.

8. Exhale, draw the belly in and up, and press back into *Downward Dog*. Ground your hands and feet into the floor, press the tops of the thighs back, and extend the whole spine. Take three long, deep breaths....

9. Inhale and step the right foot forward to your right thumb, returning to a *High Lunge*.

10. Exhale, step the left foot forward to join the right, and come into *Standing Forward Fold or Standing Half Forward Bend*.

11. Inhale, ground through the feet, soften the knees a little, firm the belly, and sweep the arms out and up, returning to the *Upward Salute*.

12. Exhale, press the palms lightly together and draw them down the midline, returning to *Mountain* pose. Take a few moments to center and reconnect to your breath before doing the whole sequence on the other side.

The second goal of meditation is to connect with the spiritual world and both gain information about your purpose in life and receive healing energy from it, as was described at the beginning of the chapter. It is this type of meditation that allows us to build a relationship with our spirit guide(s) and build confidence in the spiritual world. The stronger our relationship with the spiritual world and its inhabitants, the greater the reliance we can place on them to carry us through the most difficult times we will face in our lives.

There are numerous such guided meditations that can assist us on this path of discovery and renewal. I highly recommend a guided mediation from Lene. You can find it on-line at GLZ.org in the journal issue 4/2020, entitled "Meditation Guidance." It takes time to establish a practice in meditation, specifically feeling and smelling the spiritual realm and being able to visualize its beauty. But with practice, many wonders await as Lene describes at the beginning of the chapter.

CHAPTER 10
Raising Children

It is a pity, because today more than ever the despair over the apparent meaninglessness of life has become an urgent and topical issue on a worldwide scale. Our industrial society is out to satisfy each and every need, and our consumer society even creates some needs to satisfy them. The most important need, however, the basic need for meaning, remains-more often than not-ignored and neglected. And it is so "important" because once a man's will to meaning is fulfilled, he becomes able and capable of suffering, of coping with frustrations and tensions, and—if need be—he is prepared to give his life. Just look at the various political resistance movements throughout history and in present times. On the other hand, if man's will to meaning is frustrated, he is equally inclined to take his life, and he does so in the midst, and in spite, of all the welfare and affluence surrounding him. Just look at the staggering suicide figures in typical welfare states such as Sweden and Austria. —Viktor Frankl[39]

AS PARENTS, VIKTOR FRANKL PAINTS a vivid picture of the stakes. Do we raise resilient children, able to face an ever-changing future? Or do we let them fall into despair?

A significant consequence of the Two-World Hypothesis is we cannot count on our genetics to be the only determining factor on our child as they come into the world. Besides genetics, they come into life with spiritual gifts,

---

[39] Viktor E. Frankl, *The Will to Meaning: Foundations and Applications of Logotherapy* (expanded ed., with a new afterword by the author) (Meridian, 1988), 167.

past-life memories, and possibly karma. It is during the early formative years that we as parents can have the greatest impact on the child's development, affecting their entire lifetime. It is the perfect time to start building resilience by helping them to find meaning.

The goal of parents should be to act as role model, coach, and cheerleader.

Role model is the most important of the three tasks of parents. We cannot live the lives of our children and need to accept that this is the most beneficial for our children's lives from day one. This will be beneficial for the entire family. Also, the more virtues we can demonstrate to them, the greater the chance they will mimic this behavior and learn these virtues. This is not always the case, as we will see. Depending on the child's disposition, they may choose to reject the example of the parents. And guess what, it is not the fault of the parent; coaches can only do their job, the players need to do theirs also.

The coach should be looking for the unique skills of the children and providing opportunities for them to demonstrate their capabilities. The coach encourages them to stretch themselves, exploring their limits and building resilience. By focusing early on the strengths and aptitudes of the child, the coach can help the child to learn what success feels like, while exploring what is meaningful to them. In addition, it is easier to recover from defeat in an area of strength rather than weakness. Only after learning how to succeed and how to recover from failure should we encourage the child to attempt the tasks they are not so good at. A wise man once told me: "If you spend all your time working on weaknesses, then all you can ever be is mediocre. But if you spend time on your gifts, you can be extraordinary."

This is not as easy as it sounds. There are social pressures and systems in place that force children to be equally proficient at many tasks. If a child's strengths do not lie within the social norms, it is difficult for them to learn how to be successful in the way I describe. And even if they have learned to be successful in areas not valued by society, they can still be left with a feeling of failure in the areas that most friends are successful.

The role of the coach can be awkward when the skills of your child lie outside your own expertise. But that is what other coaches are for, and a good coach can take cues from other scouts. If someone else uncovers a talent in your child, be ready to outsource that part of your coaching. They only have two parents, but they can benefit from many coaches. There are some skills our children have that we might not be aware of ourselves or even do not appreciate. This is where the role of cheerleader comes in; cheer them on, and push them to be the best they can be.

Early Childhood Development

From the first day of a child's life, they are capable of learning, much more than many realize. Yes, their brains are not developed, but their spirit is fully aware and conscious. The only real problem is babies have not yet developed the ability to express their consciousness. In her life's work, Caroline Eliacheff demonstrated how much babies learn in their early months and discovered how to listen to them by learning to read their body language.[40]

I can highly suggest going through the Hoffman Process before having children. This is a way of finding out what your parents did wrong in raising you and making sure you do not pass on the same mistakes to your children. We retain many unconscious behaviors that are a product of our upbringing. No one cannot eliminate them all, but it is prudent to be aware of them before you inadvertently pass them on to your kids.

The life's work of Bob Hoffman studied the impact of the parents' behaviors on children in the formative years. Most people that I know who have gone through the Hoffman training come away with the same question: "Why isn't this vital information taught in school to every potential parent?" Why don't we learn that the first five years of life are the most impressionable, and that the behaviors developed in this time period are hard to overcome?

It is the second part of the question that is most impactful. What we teach our children in the first five years of life has the greatest lasting effect on

---

[40] Caroline Eliacheff, *Das Kind, das eine Katze sein wollte: Psychoanalytische Arbeit mit Säuglingen und Kleinkindern* (Dtv, 2013).

their lives. It is not reading and mathematics, but social behaviors and emotional stability that are fortified here. These build the foundation for successful networking and relationship building that we now know are more critical for lifelong success than academic expertise.

> We are all born with five main emotions: fear, anger, grief, joy, and love. When expressed in a healthy way, fear protects us, anger allows us to set healthy boundaries, and grief enables us to shed healing tears over our losses. Joy provides the enthusiasm to live life with passion, while love provides the comfort of positive relationships. These make up our essential emotions, driving the myriad of feelings we may experience throughout the day.

> However, these emotions can become blocked and unhealthy, and the one that suffers most is love. The word emotion is derived from the Latin *emovere*, meaning to move or emit motion. If we become e-motion-less, we stop moving, and our feelings stay stuck. It's easy to imagine how this might happen to a child. Not wanting to endure the pain of being left alone or feeling unloved, the young child defends itself by closing off some of its emotions. The layers become thicker as the years go on, until we find, in our adult years, that they have become almost impenetrable.[41]

The founder of *All Kinds of Minds*, Dr. Mel Levine, is an inspiration and not only for parents with "difficult children." He has specialized in "learning disabled children" and admits he has yet to find one. He says it is a failure of parents and teachers to recognize the diverse talents that children are given that causes them to assign labels. He tells his patients that each child has a toolbox with various tools, but sometimes we are not allowed to use our entire toolbox, as for instance in school.[42] For example, kinesthetic learners

---

[41] Viktor E. Frankl, quoted in Laurence, *The Hoffman Process*, 99.
[42] Mel Levine M.D., *A Mind at a Time* (Simon & Schuster, 2002).

are disadvantaged in classical classroom settings where they are unable to use movement to assist in their analytical process.

Levine's methodology and strategies are successful with *"learning disabled"* children, but they are equally valuable for *"normal"* children. There are actually many techniques used for the *disabled* that should be used in general for all children, such as music therapy. Certain music has positive effects on brain function and can be beneficial for mood disorders. The reason behind this positive impact has been demonstrated in the work of Dr. Emoto and Blanche Merz who independently discovered the healing of certain music composers.

There is a deep spiritual meaning behind *All Kinds of Minds*. A vast diversity exists in the spiritual world. It is filled with a wide range of talented spirits. Our society does not place value on many of these talents, but we still can help children to use their spiritual gifts and be successful in life.

The Author's Journey

When our daughter was born, I asked my wife to promise me that we would support our child, regardless of what she wanted to do. This is the hardest commitment to remain true to but turned out to be the most rewarding. This does not mean you let them do anything they want, but you let them lead in choosing their paths in life, even if you know it will "end badly," but then there is no bad ending to failure if they learn from it. The first major choice our daughter made was at the age of three—she wanted a house with a pool, so we agreed as long as she learned how to swim first. By the age of eight she was a top swimmer in every stroke. The key is holding them to their choice over time while making sure they know the consequences of the choice, because in the end, it is not the destination that is important, life is about the journey. By the time she was thirteen, swimming had served its purpose. She realized that although she was highly skilled, it was not meaningful to her, yet it was the only school-wide recognition she received.

When she was six, she wanted to join the choir that her friend sang in. We told her: "If you join the choir, you need to practice daily, go to practice every Friday night, and go sing in church for two hours on Sunday." Neither of us can sing, so this was not an activity that we could coach, so we became cheerleaders and got to know her new coach. Singing opened the door to many other fulfilling pursuits.

Don't be afraid to let them go as early as fourteen. If you have not demonstrated your values to them by that time, you won't have much luck doing it in the teenage years. We let our daughter pursue a Hollywood career at fourteen, and supported her emancipation, so she could live on her own to do this. (We lived three thousand miles away.) By seventeen she had enough, including the greatest college essay you could ask for. The beauty of letting them go for it at a young age is they will never have any regrets. She met actresses who went to college only to find out it was not for them at the age of thirty. What are a few years when they are young?

Raising Young Souls

It takes great patience and understanding to raise a young soul. Even with this, the chance of becoming a "successful parent" to a young soul is dauntingly slight.

Summary

I cannot summarize the role of a parent any better than Joey Guald when he founded the Hyde School and its ten priorities.

- **Truth over Harmony** – We all want honest families. We also want everyone to get along. Which do we want more? This priority calls upon parents to put the weight of their feet on the side of truth.
- **Principles over Rules** – We tend to apply rules when things are starting to spin out of control (e.g., "There is no eating in *that* room, either!"). Rules must be guided by deep principles.
- **Attitude over Aptitude** – Schools, families, and society in general would be much healthier if we valued attitude over aptitude, effort

over ability, and character over talent. Parents often send the message that successful outcomes are more important than honest efforts.

- **Set High Expectations and Let Go of the Outcomes** – Discipline alone will not properly raise our children. We need to aim high with our expectations and resist "lowering the bar" when we sense that our children are having difficulty achieving success. Letting go of the outcome allows our children to take responsibility for their actions.
- **Value Success and Failure** – Today's parents have a hard time letting their children fail. Success is important, but failure can teach powerful lifelong lessons leading to profound personal growth.
- **Allowing Obstacles to Become Opportunities** – We can get caught up in trying to "fix" our children's problems (e.g., disagreements with their teachers and coaches) instead of seeing the potential for positive learning opportunities.
- **Taking Hold and Letting Go** – It is hard to watch our children struggle with life's challenges. When should we step in? When should we step away? This is one of the toughest parenting dilemmas.
- **Create a Character Culture** – This priority can help parents create an atmosphere of character in the home through the application of a three-point plan: a daily job, a weekly family meeting, and a concept called "mandatory fun."
- **Humility to Ask for and Accept Help** – While parents focus on helping their children, many avoid asking others for help. Consequently, they raise children who do not ask for help.
- **Inspiration: Job #1** – Regardless of what they might say or do, teens share a deep yearning to be inspired by their parents. Ironically, we will not inspire our children with our achievements. We best inspire them when we share our struggles, reach for our best, and model daily character.[43]

---

[43] Laura Gauld and Malcolm Gauld, "10 Priorities," *The Biggest Job We'll Ever Have: The Hyde School Program for Character-Based Education and Parenting* (Scribner, 2003), 57–78.

Enlightened parenting has the greatest social payoff, so when I exhausted my knowledge, I reached out to an expert in the field of early childhood development and asked for her expertise. Dr. Anjum Babukhan is the managing director of Glendale Academy, author of ABCs of Brain Compatible Learning and TEDx Speaker. Dr. Babukhan is an awarding-winning educationist, empowering trainer, and lifelong learner. She provides key insights for educators, parents and lifelong learners to navigate education in the 21st century. Please read her perspective to *"Develop the multi-faceted gifts of each child to unleash their full spectrum of human potential"* in Appendix 6.

CHAPTER 11

The Spiritual Battle

Just a few minutes ago a spiritual being came and sat down across from me. When I wrote the above-mentioned introduction on my notepad, the spirit says:

"What, you are writing a book?"

"Yes, Conversations with the Deceased is the intended title."

"I like that, people have no idea."

Now I breathe in healing-light from heaven, so that I may be able to continue to see him and to speak with him.

"You look beautiful, do that again." he says.

He has a pleasant aura. It is the same with humans, loving people have pleasant auras, but others make us feel tired. Their aura is not pleasant to us.

Now I ask the spirit across from me:

"What were you in your human life?"

"Nothing special. An office worker."

"Where did you live?"

"In P——"

"Why did not you go to your spiritual, heavenly level with your guardian spirit?"

"I was there, I did not like it. Guardian spirit you say?"

"Yes, every human being has a protective angel, with which one should speak to often during their life on earth. And in the case of death and its transition, this is particularly important."

"No one told us."

Now I am doing light-healing exercises again and looking at the springtime nature.

"Don't you want to know more about me? Him there (pointing beside me to my guardian spirit) said I should tell you my story."

"Okay, how did you experience dying?"

"Do not know, I suddenly stood beside my body and I watched them carry it away. Then I went to my wife. She did not notice me. She was sad and very exhausted. We were not very good together. I do not care. So what. That's all over. Now I'm going to hang around here. I know that something else will come. I do not care." This spirit wore the clothes of someone who goes to the office every day, but without a blazer.[44]

IN THE FIRST CHAPTER, I went through the possible spiritual battles that could impact your life and the lives of your loved ones. So far, in the second half of this book I have made recommendations for strengthening your inner light, increasing your spiritual strength as it were. This is done

---

[44] Elisabeth Vonderau, "Im Zug," in *Begegnungen mit verstorbenen Erlebnisberichte* by August Von Goethe (Literaturverlag, 2017), 38 (Translated from the German by Google).

to prepare you as much as possible for the most arduous tasks you have to face in life.

We cannot effectively help ourselves or others without being strong, both spiritually and physically. The spiritual strength that we speak of is both acquired through works of goodness and through spiritual knowledge or enlightenment—knowing your own limitations and the laws of the spiritual world. This is imperative to make sure that your efforts are effective, while not making matters worse or exposing yourself to the evil spiritual world. An example of this type of mishap was recounted in chapter 1, from a patient of Dr. Fiore who inadvertently invited a foreign spirit to share her life. As I describe in the previous chapter on raising children, we cannot live another's life for them; no matter how loving the intension, it is destructive for all parties.

There are many spirits around us. Some are connected to the place that we live, while others are connected to people from this lifetime or from past lifetimes. Some are benign observers as described at the beginning of the chapter. Here is a specific example of how this might appear in your life or a loved one. A friend of mine, Will, has suffered from schizophrenia his whole life. It took him some time to realize that the voices were not "in his head" and that the medications prescribed for him were not effective to drown out the voices. Through his study, he realizes the voices he is hearing are from evil or vengeful spirits. He recently wrote to me:

> Sorry, I have been having a very difficult time with these entities. I have almost completely stopped writing. I do not have any self-will for survival[.] I feel like I'm losing control. They have powerful, if not absolute control over my life.
>
> It is like a nightmare that you can't wake up from. I don't sleep much. The attacks from when I do try to sleep are terrifying and extremely painful. They have caused trauma which why I tremble and have difficulty speaking, sometimes, panic attacks, flashbacks....
>
> This shouldn't happen.

For the last ten years my life has been like a supernatural horror movie. Not even the most depraved mind could come up with the torture, torment, and scenarios set up by these demonic beings. It wouldn't surprise me if it was Satan himself, maybe Samuel and Lilith, given the experiences.

I often cannot tell the difference between my life and Hell. At this point does it really matter. It feels like Hell. I can only hope that this journey through Hell arrives in Heaven.

However, the pain and sickness is overwhelming. Although, I feel at peace. I also am weaker than ever. I have no choice but to trust my fate to God. I have all but given up trying to fight. After all, I am hardly a match for what seems like an innumerable number of ancient spirits.

I would like to tell all about everything I've been through, but sadly this world would probably label [it] a work of fiction. The journey has been profound, but frankly I am tired.

As Will says, it is hard for anyone without such an affliction to understand what he is going through. Rushing in to help, without proper training, could result in getting caught in the same nightmare that he is trapped in. So let us first look at the spiritual laws that might be in play in Will's life.

The first law to examine is *an eye for an eye* and its corollary the *right of retribution*. This means these spirits may be exacting some type of revenge on Will. It could be from the spirit of someone in this lifetime, or from a previous incarnation. If this is the case, then the only one who can rectify the situation is Will. In this case, if someone tried to exorcise the spirits, they could not overcome the *right of retribution*. Any effect would be fleeting. The most effective contribution that a third party could offer is twofold. The first is to support Will morally and spiritually. A person in a spiritual battle often feels alone and can become depressed. In addition, they might be surrounded by people who do not believe them; thus, they are fighting a battle on two fronts. This is where the spiritually enlightened can provide support. Many of those who suffer from lost or evil spirits have been told by parents and doctors that they are crazy and the spirits do not exist. By giving our unconditional support, they can find the strength to concentrate on their spiritual battle.

There are a few things we can do to support Will spiritually, but the most important is to send him as much spiritual light or positive energy as possible, in any way you are comfortable. Furthermore, eliminating the negative energy he is receiving from friends and family is a good start.

Here are two effective prayers for this type of situation from the spiritual teacher Josef, who teaches in conjunction with Lene at GL Zürich.

Prayer for Health

> Loving Father,
> take away all the pain
> from our sick friends.
> Heal their body and soul,
> fill them with grace, bless them.
> God be honored and praised,
> and glory be to God and Christ.
> (Josef)[45]

Prayer for Health and Courage

> We ask you, O gracious God,
> look after our sick friends and bless them,
> for they are healed through your blessing.
> Comfort all our friends
> who require comfort and courage.
> Send your angels of peace into every home
> so that peace may spread further.

---

[45] Gebete, Pro Beatrice, 2008, 62 (Translated from the German by Google).

Bless this whole community, bless this earth.
(Josef)[46]

You will recognize a second spiritual law reflected in the prayers that I have included in this book: *Thy will be done.* You will find that these prayers are as general as possible, and they do not demand a specific outcome. Focusing on the process and letting go of the outcome is recommended in many areas, and it is just as important in prayer. The energy created by such a prayer can be used by the spiritual world without having strings attached to it. For example, if it is God's will that Will suffers, these prayers allow him to be supported in his suffering, including all those around him.

The other aspect of the *eye for an eye* law is something that the sufferer alone can do, and as a third party, we can remind them of it. This is what I wrote to Will to explain his part in his spiritual battle.

+ The evil spirits connected to you are connected through hate. The only way to overcome hate is through forgiveness. I like to think of what Jesus said: "Father, forgive them, for they know not what they do." In addition, I have two suggested prayers below that are part of my daily routine for the dark spirits and lost souls.

Prayer for Lost Souls

Gracious and merciful God,
have mercy on the poor souls.
Deliver them, free them from their pain.
Adored are you and praised,
you merciful God.
Your will be done
in heaven and everywhere.
(Josef)[47]

---

[46] Gebete, Pro Beatrice, 2008, 65 (Translated from the German by Google).
[47] Gebete, Pro Beatrice, 2008, 72 (Translated from the German by Google).

Prayer for Dark Spirits

> Good God,
> send out an angel of light
> and an angel of solace,
> that the poor souls
> may be led out of the darkness.
> Take all the good deeds of my friends as thanks,
> praise and honor to you.
> And set them free, good God.
> We all urgently beg you.
> (Josef)[48]

+ Another way to overcome these unvirtuous beings is to raise yourself above them. The darkness fears the light and if you can lighten your soul, they will shun it and you. This is not easy work of course. It requires more than prayer—it requires good works. This means doing good deeds and having good thoughts for those around you.

If the suffering person can shift their attention from their spiritual battle to helping those around them, they can eventually achieve relief from the evil spirits. There are many experiences that Will can draw from this spiritual battle that can be used to help others.

The third law that could be at play is *likeness attracts*. I alluded to this in the second recommendation I gave to Will above. A person with evil intentions will attract similar spirits, and these spirits can easily influence the person in question. If they have addictions, these can be exploited by spirits of people who died with the same addiction. Since addiction is a spiritual disorder, it persists after death, as does the desire. The only way they can experience the same "high" is by temporarily possessing this weak-willed person as described in chapter 1. The treatment for such a case is the same as I prescribed for Will above, in addition to a twelve-step program offered by AA or NA.

---

[48] Gebete, Pro Beatrice, 2008, 73 (Translated from the German by Google).

The fourth law that could be at play is *an open invitation as a part of free will*. The situation described at the end of chapter 1 is common, where people inadvertently or unknowingly issue an open invitation to either evil spirits or familiar spirits. The graphic at the end of chapter 1 visualizes the various possibilities. Whether the invitation was done through a visit to a hypnotist, participation in a séance, or a wicca ceremony, the door has been opened, and you need to close it. There are two actions you need to take. The first action is to rescind all invitations you have given for spirits, including humans, to enter your aura. I suggest saying the following regularly until you totally believe it.

> I rescind all invitations to all beings, issued consciously or unconsciously.

The second action is to use the techniques described in chapters 7 through 9 to strengthen your aura. The stronger your own spiritual light, the harder it is for unwanted spirits to influence you.

At this point, we need to transition to the strategies you can use to protect yourself. There are numerous situations where the only thing you can do is shield yourself from it. The central theme is demons—or protecting ourselves from the negative energies emanating from our fellow man. In chapter 7 we touch on the positive energy that humans can create from the research by Dr. Masaru Emoto, but he also researched the detrimental impact of negative thoughts or intentions on water and, therefore, on people. Without realizing it, we can accumulate this negative energy in our aura from people who have negative thoughts about us, our family, or our possessions. It does not have to be someone you know; there are random people who harbor jealousy, envy, and hate merely for the way you look or who they think you are. To help illustrate the impact on us, I like to visualize the Peanuts character Pigpen[49] by Charles Schulz, wandering around oblivious to the dirty (negative) energy cloud we can collect. Without a daily cleansing routine, this cloud can grow into a powerful force—a demon, capable of magnifying our own base instincts.

---

[49] https://schulzmuseum.org/explore/exhibits/behind-peanuts-pigpen/

Accumulated negative energy can be cleared with a daily meditation routine, a daily prayer ritual or even a mindful encounter with nature. Here is where it is important to mention the necessity of being mindful of all the people and spiritual beings around us and making sure to include everyone in your prayers, simply because we cannot know who might be responsible for these negative thoughts.

At some point, you may find yourself sitting or standing across from a person who is directing negative energy and thoughts at you. The simplest way is to close yourself energetically to protect yourself and not absorb the negative energy into your aura. Many people do this instinctively already by folding their arms on their chest. You can achieve the same effect by simply holding your fingertips from the right hand against the fingertips of the left hand. If you cross your ankles in addition, you have closed your body and aura off from absorbing energy.[50] Don't forget to open yourself up though when someone is sharing their love with you.

To be successful in any spiritual battle, you should maximize the light around you and minimize the darkness, utilizing any effective techniques you are comfortable with, from positive thinking to tapping into the spiritual powers in nature, prayer, and meditation.

---

[50] Choa Kok Sui, *Pranic Psychotherapy* (Institute for Inner Studies, 2000).

CHAPTER 12
Lifelong Learning

Then one of them talked to me intensively causing my fear to increase more and more. "What is it you have brought with you?", he asked resolutely. I hardly knew what to answer. What did I bring home with me? Nothing; I brought home nothing—I wasn't pleased with myself either. I didn't even know what they meant. So I countered: "Well, I possessed wealth but I had to leave it behind." And they replied: "We're not talking about transient things. Everything you've left behind is destined to perish; we're not interested in that. We're interested in the everlasting. Did you do such deeds? This is the harvest which we want to talk about." And I had to reflect: something everlasting? What did I do that was imperishable? I had no answer to give. "I did good deeds as well", I told them, but they didn't appear to be satisfied with it. And my fear increased more and more and I could hardly speak, because they became more and more aggressive and they kept on asking me more and more forcefully what I had brought across with me; I simply had no answer. And as I became rather desperate a figure suddenly approached me that immediately gave me the feeling: "This being is well disposed towards me." He had a smile on his face and held up his hands to signal the others that they should keep quiet for a while. This very nice being stood next to me and I breathed a sigh of relief—truly, because I felt much freer and thought: "At last; finally I have a helper, someone who will stand up for me!" I suddenly felt secure in the presence of this being.

Now this being spoke about my life, about my faults and about the things I had done well and my merits as well. And this being appeared to talk much less about my faults but mainly about the good deeds. I soon realized that I had a defender. Every now and then one of the others spoke a word and raised an objection, but this being kept on talking and appeared to gain the upper hand. Then the figures who had first asked about the harvest, talking to me increasingly stricter, suddenly became gentle and their countenances friendlier. What surprise and what joy! And my fear dissipated more and more. The questioning had stopped.

Then the two sides—that is, these strict beings and my defender, that's how I'll call them—began to discuss with each other and to talk about my life, resulting in a to and fro. Then they seemed to come to an agreement about my future. I was no longer able to follow their conversation. After all, I had no idea about any spiritual order and laws; everything was strange to me when they talked about reparations, reincarnation, karma, purification and so on. I knew nothing about it and couldn't reply and, as a precaution, kept quiet. My defender had acted on my behalf. Then these figures disappeared and I stood there with my defender. I had to thank him; I knelt down, kissed his hands and thanked him for freeing and helping me. And this lovely being raised me up, gave me courage and comfort saying: "Well, you did do many things wrong in your life and your harvest isn't particularly big. You'll have much to make up for." And so, this divine spirit spoke to me kindly and reminded me to be very obedient in future. He said that I would be given a certain time of adaptation, that I could rest for a while and sleep, that I could also take a look at my surroundings and admire.[51]

---

[51] "A Deathbed Experience," *The Spiritual World*, vol. 2019, no. 5: 12.

IT IS ONLY YOUR SPIRITUAL accomplishments that you carry into your next life. Therefore, I highly recommend maintaining lifelong spiritual learning. Throughout this book I have referenced researchers who devoted their lives to a specific area of spiritual health, and I have shown how to combine these achievements into a diverse methodology for enhancing spiritual and physical health. But I hope that this is only the beginning for each reader. I encourage further learning in the areas that interest you the most. Specifically, I can highly recommend taking journeys of self-discovery to open up yet undiscovered areas of spiritual learning potential.

I have been fortunate to be able to go on diverse journeys of personal discovery. The Mankind Project[52] helps to provide a missing link in modern society, and that is a lack of community recognition of adulthood by making the official transition from being a child of two parents to becoming a member of the community.

The Hoffman Process[53] helps us to overcome the spiritual trauma that we may have endured as children and carry on into adulthood. It is a reconciliation process with our parents and family. An adventure similar to Outward Bound[54] is an opportunity to connect with the spiritual energies in nature and learn about your limits and passions. These journeys are in nature, and there is no amount of study that can replace visceral learning.

No book can tell you specifically why you are here and why you have been presented with the specific challenges in your life. YPO Forum,[55] for instance, offers well-developed protocols to help explore a person's "best stuff" and discover the underlying meaning of one's life. This of course can change with time and the role that one currently fulfills, thus turning into lifelong learning. It is self-discovery that has led me to become an author,

---

[52] "Who We Are", ManKind Project, last modified 2017, https://mankindproject. org/who-we-are/.
[53] "What Is the Hoffman Process?", Hoffman Institute, last modified December 31, 2014, https://www.hoffmaninstitute.org/the-process/.
[54] "Programs", Outward Bound, accessed June 3, 2021, https://www.outwardbound. org/programs/.
[55] "Alumni Forum Services", Harvard Business School, last published April 21, 2021, https://www.alumniforums.org/.

and sharing my stories has impacted a few individuals who have similar experiences. I do not expect to reach the masses with this work. However, I can help more people by encouraging others to take their own journey, and I hope using the methodology that has been demonstrated in the *Torn between Two Worlds* series can lead to additional pioneers who can help yet others.

I would like to close with a power prayer that I can suggest adding to your daily ritual.

Almighty Father of well-being and peace, in the name of our highest prince of peace, Jesus Christ, we ask you, send out your infinite legions of peace, reconciliation and salvation, and let it flow into all human hearts and into the souls of all the rulers of this earth: Your powers of benevolence and helpfulness, your powers of modesty and forgiveness, your powers of peacefulness and heavenly faith.

Let your holy lights of mercy and compassion find their way into all beings so that salvation and freedom may work powerfully in them.

May the smoldering fire be extinguished by your heavenly dew of peace. May all dividing walls crumble into nothingness, and your heavenly goodness, heavenly strength, and heavenly wisdom be revealed to all men, because you are the invincible guard over our spirit, our soul, our body, our work and our life.

Your Holy Will, O Father, be done now and forever. (Josef)[56]

---

[56] Gebete, Pro Beatrice, 2008, 50–51 (Translated from the German by Google).

CONCLUSION

I KNOW THAT I HAVE not satisfied every reader, nor given all the answers to a few. My hope is that I have given many pause at least to question the status quo.

Seek and ye shall find, knock and the door will be opened.

The second to last spiritual law that I will leave you with is most likely the most important. But we do not really understand its importance until we turn it around. If you do not look, you will not find what you are looking for. If you do not seek for answers, you will not find them.

This is the main purpose behind self-discovery. Not until we know who we truly are, can we start asking the right questions. That is when the search can begin in earnest. For me, it wasn't until my mother noticed something in my five-year-old daughter that reminded her of me when I was five. She said to me: "Your daughter is such a loving child. She reminds me of you at that age—what happened?"

I spent many years chasing this question, *What happened to me when I was five to cause me to lose my heart?* In the end, it was not the answer to this question that was revealing; I knew it deep down. It was the search that was the most fascinating. The search for my lost childhood opened up many doors. Specifically, this journey has given me the conviction to help others with the discoveries from my journey. It has given meaning to the final law I leave with you:

Love thy neighbor as thyself.

My journey has taught me how gratifying this law can be. There have been a handful of people—like Will, mentioned in chapter 11—whom I have been able to accept as they are. For them, it was the first time in their life that someone had truly listened to and accepted their reality. This started them on their spiritual healing process and in turn gives me strength to continue.

APPENDIX 1

Final Judgment

MODERN CHRISTIANS ARE MADE FUN of for their view of the "end of the world" or "the final judgment." Some Catholics have taken it so far that they actually believe in the physical resurrection of the dead, causing many to bury their dead in a concrete cask so that the physical parts will be available for this event. Where did this thinking go astray to end up with such an illogical belief?

> It is the spirit that quickeneth; the flesh profiteth nothing: the words that I speak unto you, they are spirit, and they are life. (John 6:63)

Even at the time of Jesus, people did not understand this fundamental concept about His words: they are all spiritual in nature and have little or no relationship to the physical/material world. Origen reminds us of this often enough in his commentaries that there are so many things Jesus said, concerning His kingdom for example, that obviously had no literal interpretation. So if we examine the words of Jesus about "the final judgment" with this in mind, maybe we can find a logical explanation.

During his time of teaching, Jesus told us that the Father had given Him the authority to judge the world, including every soul on earth or in Hell (see John 6:27). He tells us that the hour is coming when all the souls will hear His voice, and He will separate them into two groups: those who earn the right to go to Heaven and those who will be sentenced in court (John 5:26–29). Many Christians take this to mean that at some point in the future all will be judged, with some going to everlasting life and the rest into eternal damnation.

But doesn't this interpretation contradict the good news from Jesus? Jesus tells us it is the will of God that none of His children be lost (see John 6:39–40; Luke 15:4–7). Jesus also tells us that He has come to save the whole world and not condemn it (John 3:17). We must consider we cannot comprehend the patience of God, and that He truly is patient enough to make sure that none of His children perish (2 Peter 3:8–9). In the parable of the prodigal son, Jesus attempts to explain the Father's patience to us. If we take Lucifer to be the prodigal son Jesus is talking about, who took his inheritance and squandered it, we can see that he now lives much worse off than any of those in Heaven. How long will it be before he comes to his senses and starts his way back to God (see Luke 15:11–31)? How long will it be before the Morning Star, Lucifer, rises in our hearts? (see Isaiah 14:12; 2 Peter 1:19)?

The early Christian teaching of the good news had a more humane explanation of the final judgment that truly allowed for all to be eventually saved. Near the end of His life, Jesus tells us that the hour has come for the world to be judged and when the king of this world will be dethroned (John 12:31–32). When He had successfully passed all His tests on earth, Jesus was ready to go down into Hell and meet His adversary face-to-face. The Bible available to us today gives little reference to the three days that Jesus spent in Hell. In John's revelation there are some references to the event, but the picture that he can tell us is not precise. From St. Fulbert of Chartres (d. 1028) we have a poetic rendition of this occurrence which is a little easier to understand than those images from John (Revelation 12:3–4, 7–9; 20:1–3):

> For Judah's Lion bursts his chains,
> crushing the serpent's head;
> and cries aloud through death's domains
> to wake the imprisoned dead.
>
> Devouring depths of hell their prey
> at his command restore;
> his ransomed hosts pursue their way
> where Jesus goes before.

If we take these images along with the parable of the sheep and goats, we can come to the following explanation of these three days in Hell. After His death on the cross, the spirit of Jesus went to Paradise (Luke 23:43) where He met the archangel Michael and his army. Jesus then led this army into Hell and conquered Lucifer. Upon His victory, Jesus passed the final judgment on Lucifer. This final judgment is to last until the world is no longer needed for the restoration of the fallen (dead). This was the new epoch prophesied in which Lucifer's (Death's) unlimited power over the inhabitants of earth and Hell was to be curtailed.

> So when this corruptible shall have put on incorruption, and this mortal shall have put on immortality, then shall be brought to pass the saying written, Death is swallowed up in victory [Isaiah 25:8]. O death, where is thy sting? O grave, where is thy victory? [Hosea 13:14]. The sting of death is sin; and the strength of sin is the law. But thanks be to God, which giveth us the victory through our Lord Jesus Christ. (1 Corinthians 15:54–57)

After the final judgment, Jesus gathered His sheep and sorted them out. Those who had proven their loyalty to Him and God were allowed to follow Him into Heaven and eternal life, like Abraham and Moses. Those who have not yet shown their loyalty to Him are now subject to the conditions of the final judgment, under which they must actively choose to follow Jesus and prove their loyalty to Him on earth (see Matthew 25:31–46) The current interpretation of the Bible is that this judgment will last an eternity. It is impossible for a mortal to comprehend a spiritual eternity, but the judgment will certainly last a human eternity, since the remaining useful life of the earth will stretch for billions of years, and the prodigal son finally returns.

APPENDIX 2

Origen of Alexandria: A Prophet?

Introduction

ORIGEN WAS BORN IN AD 185 or 186 and died in approximately 254, probably at the age of seventy after suffering persecution and imprisonment. It is widely agreed he was an extraordinary man. He began earning a living as a teacher at the age of eighteen and demonstrated exceptional character. The 1911 Encyclopedia states:

As a boy he showed evidence of remarkable talents....

His character was as transparent as his life was blameless; there are few church fathers whose biography leaves so pure an impression on the reader.

He could not have been what he was unless two generations before him had labored at the problem of finding an intellectual expression and a philosophic basis for Christianity (Justin, Tatian, Athenagoras, Pantaenus, Clement). But their attempts, in comparison with his, are like a schoolboy's essays beside the finished work of a master.[57]

His literary productivity was unmatched in ancient times, and if the estimate of six thousand[58] various works is accurate, it is still an excellent achievement in modern times. But he was unique in a more vital area: his application of what we know today as the scientific method to the study

---

[57] The 1911 Encyclopedia states, http://encyclopedia.jrank.org/ORC_PAI/ ORIGEN_c_185_c_254_.html
[58] "St. Epiphanius declared that Origen had written 6000 works—scrolls of undoubted value and of varied lengths." www.copticchurch.net/topics/patrology/ schoolofalex2/chapter02.html

of scripture. It was his work on the Hexapla[59] which exemplifies his in-depth knowledge of and logical approach to scripture. Together with this unsurpassed foundation and the guidance of Greek philosophy, he was able to uncover the mysteries of the most spiritual Gospel. His thirty-two volume commentary on the Gospel of John was the pinnacle of his work.

Two Camps

Most seem to agree on Origen's industrious life, but there is considerable controversy about the truth (orthodoxy) of all his teachings. This was a problem in his day, exemplified by his need to leave Alexandria, and it continues today. The difficulty centers on Origen's spirituality. His highest goal was to extract the deeper spiritual meaning from Scripture, and as we will see, this causes extensive conflict for those who do not share his spiritual view, which they therefore label "mysticism" or "speculation." This verdict is given by those who do not understand Origen's allegorical methodology and do not share his broad scientific basis. Henry Crouzel's description of the various views of prophecy exemplifies the difficulty accepting the allegorical interpretations from certain authors.

So the mystery is food; it is also a wine, rejoicing the soul. (Origene et la 'connaissance mystique', pp. 184–197) The origin of this theme is found in the Jewish theologian Philo. It constitutes for that author the "oxymoron" of "sober drunkenness." However, between Philo's "sober drunkenness" and Origen's, there is one capital difference, already explained in connection with his exegesis. Origen is opposed to the Montanist conception of the prophetic ecstasy as unconsciousness or sacred madness, a conception that is not absent from certain texts of Philo. If, for Origen, the drunkenness occasioned by the wine of the True Vine "takes one out of the human" (Comfn I, 30 (33), 206), only the bad wine of false doctrine "takes one out of the intellect" (Homfr (Latin) II, 8 (GCS VIII)). An ecstasy that would

---

[59] Catholic Encyclopedia: "Hexapla: The name given to Origen's edition of the Old Testament in Hebrew and Greek, the most colossal critical production of antiquity." http://www.newadvent.org/cathen/07316a.htm

be unconscious is for Origen the sign the demon is present, manifest in the evil passions that warp, cloud and enslave the intellect.[60]

Below are some keys to the opposing viewpoints:

Origen: A Heretic

The widely held belief is that Origen was a synthesizer of the teachings that came before him, taking what he learned from Greek philosophy and integrating it with early Christian teaching, building on the foundation created by Clement and under the influence of the Stoics. With this newly formed basis, he became overconfident and constructed speculations which were not supported by scripture. He did not have strong evidence of these specific teachings, and the remaining writings available today do not properly support the teachings. Jean Daniélou praises Origen as truly grand:

In the course of our investigations, Origen has come before us in several guises, one after another—as an active Christian, as a learned exegete, as a philosophical genius, as a great master of the spiritual life. We may have been inclined to believe that every new side of him we discovered was the main one. That is the way of it with great men: they are equally adept at all the possible ways of being great.[61]

But the writer fails to grasp the whole of Origen's teaching and asks the reader to discard that which is speculative and has been since declared heretical.

The perishable elements in his theology of the Bible, the things he derived from the culture of his time—the allegorical methods of interpretation he borrowed from Philo and the gnostics—in no way lessen the value of his work as a whole.[62]

---

[60] H. Crouzel, *Origen*, trans. A. S. Worral (Edinburgh: T.& T. Clark, 1998), 129.
[61] Jean Daniélou, *Origen* (New York: Sheed and Ward, 1955), 310.
[62] Daniélou, *Origen*, 311

The Anathematism by the Emperor Justinian in AD 543 and its ratification at the Fifth Ecumenical Council in Constantinople in 553 were justly pronounced. This was done to stop all the radical sects which had formed on the basis of the "speculations" of Origen, allowing the "true" Christianity to flourish. The teachings condemned by the Fifth Ecumenical Council were not actually the teachings of Origen, since there is little to no support for them in his remaining works. Rufinus was given the task of translating some of Origen's works into Latin but said he often had to change the texts given to him because they were not the words of Origen. He says in the preface to his translation of Origen's Commentary on the Epistle to the Romans:

Although I wanted to touch along the coastline of a tranquil shore in my small boat and draw out tiny fish from the pools of the Greeks, you compel me, brother Heraclius, [1] to unfurl the sails for the high seas and, once I had set aside the task I had to translate the homilies [2] Adamantius [3] wrote in his old age, you persuade us to set forth in our language his fifteen books in which he discussed Paul's Letter to the Romans.

In these books, as he pursues the Apostle's thought, he is taken out into such a deep sea that anyone who follows him out there encounters enormous fear lest he be overwhelmed as much by the greatness of his thoughts as by the immensity of the waves. [4] Moreover you do not consider the fact that my breath is too weak to fill up such a magnificent trumpet of eloquence. The greatest difficulty of all, however, was that the books themselves have been tampered with. [5] For some of the volumes of the work are missing from the libraries of nearly everyone-indeed, I am unsure how this came about. To fill in these things and restore complete continuity to the Latin work does not come from my natural talent but, just as you who demand these things believe, probably by God's favor. And yet, lest I be spared any labors, you add that I am supposed to abridge this entire fifteen-volume work, a Greek text which has reached the length of some forty thousand lines or more, and, if possible, compress it to half the space. [6] These instructions were hard enough, as if imposed by a man who seems unwilling to appreciate the work load involved. Nevertheless I shall set out in the hope that by your prayers the things which seem to me to be humanly impossible might become possible as God assists me. But now, with your permission, let us listen to Origen himself, as he composes the Preface of the work at hand. [M833]ⁱ

Rufinus says in the Epilogue to his translation of Origen's Commentary on the Epistle to the Romans:

But I, who defer more to my conscience than to my name, even if I seem to add some things and fill in what is missing and abbreviate what is too long, [7] do not think it right, however, to steal the title from him who laid the foundations of the work and supplied the material for the construction of the building. Of course let it be left to the reader's discretion, when he has tested the work, to ascribe the work's merit to whom he wants. For our purpose is not to seek the readers' applause but a harvest of those who make progress.[63]

Rufinus is perceived by many to have been an admirer of Origen, but when you examine his comments closely, it is probable that Rufinus did not truly understand Origen's teaching. From the fragments of writing which we possess from Origen, we know that he does not use superfluous language, and it would be hard to imagine condensing his well-thought-out and well-documented commentaries without losing significant insight to his philosophy.

Origen is often referred to as a humanist, due to his unusually friendly theology. His humanistic tendencies emanate from his personality and his pure spirit—his love for humanity—and not through a rigorous study of the scriptures.

Origen: A Prophet

Origen has been called a "diamond," like the prophet Ezekiel (Ezekiel 3:9), and it is suggested that Origen was one of the teachers promised by

---

[63] "Preface and Epilogue to the Translation of Origen's Commentary on the Epistle to the Romans", Fathers of the Church, accessed June 3, 2021, https://www.catholicculture.org/

Jesus (Matthew 23:34). Origen brought new spiritual teachings, which were in harmony with the truths taught by Plato, Pythagoras, Homer, and Solomon.[64] With his scientific analysis of the main versions of the Old Testament, he could extract the original spiritual meanings that existed in their original form, as written by the Yahwehist (Solomon), before the Jewish priests rewrote them in the third century BC. The teachings condemned by Justinian were truly the core teachings of Origen. He needed to destroy this spiritual (humanistic) belief, and the freedoms which it brings, to maintain worldly power over the Roman Empire. In the Apocalypse of Peter it was foreseen that the leaders of this world would successfully use those who call themselves "men of God" to maintain power over the "enlightened ones" for long periods:

"And there shall be others of those who are outside our number who name themselves bishop and also deacons, as if they have received their authority from God. They bend themselves under the judgment of the leaders. Those people are dry canals."

But I said, "I am afraid because of what you have told me, that indeed little are, in our view, the counterfeit ones, indeed, that there are multitudes that will mislead other multitudes of living ones, and destroy them among themselves. And when they speak your name they will be believed."

The Savior said, "For a time determined for them in proportion to their error they will rule over the little ones. And after the completion of the error, the never-aging one of the immortal understanding shall become young, and they (the little ones) shall rule over those who are their rulers. The root of their error he shall pluck out, and he shall put it to shame so that it shall be manifest in all the impudence which it has assumed to itself. And such ones shall become unchangeable, O Peter."[65]

Justinian is credited with rewriting and simplifying Roman law, but had he done this in a Christian manner, he would have built the two highest laws

---

[64] R. Sträuli, *Origenes der Diamantene* (Zurich: ABZ Verlag, 1987).
[65] Apocalypse of Peter (VII 79,20 to 80,25).

taught by Jesus (Matthew 22:36–40) into the fabric of the law, and not doing the contrary.

Fortunately for us, Justinian's clerics had to write the edict so precisely that, in effect, they actually preserved Origen's true teaching within it.[66] These key spiritual teachings of Origen posed the greatest threat to the formation of the church's powerful eternal damnation dogma, so they were specifically destroyed. The loss of almost all his thirty-two volume commentary on the Gospel of John removed the logical foundation for his vast spiritual knowledge, which disproves the eternal damnation dogma of the church. The entire loss of the ten books of the Stromata meant the loss of a logical reconciliation between his Christianity and Ionian Greek philosophy; thus, logic and reason were removed as a requirement for the interpretation of scripture and replaced by mystery.

His theology is inherently friendly to humans because it is God's will. As Professor John Nash has recently shown in his Nobel Prize–winning work, a competitive environment in which everyone does what is best for themselves and simultaneously the best for others is far more efficient and stable than when each does only the best for themselves; as once theorized in both Friedman's economic model and Darwin's evolution model. Nash shows that the central tendency of the world in which we live is not neutral (chaotic) but clearly good. He has shown the commandment given to us by Jesus, "Love thy neighbor as thyself," is inherent in the laws of nature. This tendency for goodness is observed both in long-term positive developments in humanity and beautification of nature over the long run.

For Origen, God patiently teaches all His children through multiple tests on earth until each has been fully restored to Him. In Origen's Commentary on John 8:47 he describes the broad continuum that currently exists from demons, to men not of God, to men partially of God, to the Son of Man, and on to God. He defines the criteria of overcoming the "spirit of slavery" and beginning to learn the word of God through a "spirit of adoption" until one

---

[66] A. Harnack, *History of Dogma*, trans. N. Buchanan (Wipf & Stock Publishers, 2000), volume 3, 186.

has heard all the words of God and become perfect in every way, therefore achieving Divine Love.

And consider if it is possible, in consequence of the statement, "We know in part, and we prophesy in part," (Cf. 1 Cor 13.9) for such a one to say, "And we are sons of God in part"? And again, "When that which is perfect has come, and that which is in part has been abolished," (Cf. 1 Cor 13.10) can one say that which is perfect in regard to becoming a son of God will come when that which is in part for one to have become a son of God is abolished?[67]

Examining the Evidence

Origen tells us that with a learned logic and reason from the study of mathematics and geometry, and with the knowledge of the Ionian Greek philosophy (love of wisdom), we are ready to address the true meaning of the Scriptures.[68] His application of this technique to the versions of the Bible at his time allowed him to not only find errors in the Greek translation, but also to find the censored passages removed from the Hebrew.[69] We must use these strict prerequisites to examine his remaining teachings and those of his students to rediscover that which was incorrectly translated and completely censored from his vast body of knowledge. In this spirit, I will attempt to examine each of the points of "The Anathematism of the Emperor Justinian against Origen"[ii] to find a logical explanation for the above-mentioned diametrically opposed opinions of Origen's teaching.

Point 1: "Whoever says or thinks that human souls pre-existed, i.e., that they had previously been spirits and holy powers, but that, satiated with the vision of God, they had turned to evil, and in this way the divine love in them had died out (*apyugeisas*) and they had therefore become souls (*yukas*) and had been condemned to punishment in bodies, shall be anathema."

---

[67] Origen, "Commentary on the Gospel According to John, Books 13-32", trans. Ronald E. Heine, (Catholic University of America Press, 1993), 269.
[68] Letter of Origen to Gregory, http://www.earlychristianwritings.com/text/origen-gregory.html
[69] Letter of Origen to Africanus, http://www.newadvent.org/fathers/0414.htm

Contra-Origen: Adam was the first man or soul to inhabit the earth and, with the help of Eve, violated God's laws in the garden of Eden. "And Adam called his wife's name Eve; because she was the mother of all living" (Genesis 3:20). As the mother of the living, all have inherited the sin from her. S. Harent explains the inheritance of sin from the first-born human, Adam.

Original sin may be taken to mean: (1) the sin that Adam committed; (2) a consequence of this first sin, the hereditary stain with which we are born on account of our origin or descent from Adam. From the earliest times the latter sense of the word was more common, as may be seen by St. Augustine's statement: "the deliberate sin of the first man is the cause of original sin" (De nupt. et concup., II, xxvi, 43). It is the hereditary stain that is dealt with here. As to the sin of Adam we have not to examine the circumstances in which it was committed nor make the exegesis of the third chapter of Genesis.[70]

The church's position is that souls are either at one with God, their Creator, or being tormented in Hell for their wickedness, waiting for the great day of judgment. From his paper "Origen and the Final Restoration: A Question of Heresy," M.C. Steenberg summarizes the church's position on souls, both divine and corrupt.

The bodies of men, after death, return to dust, and see corruption: (Gen. 3:19, Acts 13:36) but their souls, which neither die nor sleep, having an immortal subsistence, immediately return to God who gave them: (Luke 23:43, Eccles. 12:7) the souls of the righteous, being then made perfect in holiness, are received into the highest heavens (paradise) where they (are with Christ and) behold the face of God, in light and glory, waiting for the full redemption of their bodies. (Heb. 12:23, 2 Cor. 5:1, 6, 8, Phil. 1:23, Acts 3:21, Eph. 4:10, Rom. 8:23) And the souls of the wicked are cast into hell, where they remain in torments and utter darkness, reserved to the judgement of the great day. (Luke 16:23, 24, Acts 1:25, Jude 6, 7, 1 Pet. 3:19)

---

[70] S. Harent, "Original Sin", accessed June 3, 2021, https://www.ewtn.com/catholicism/library/original-sin-10353

Beside these two places, for souls separated from the bodies, the Scripture acknowledgeth none.[71]

Pro-Origen: One of the meanings of death for Origen was the cooling of the heart to God by His children and their Fall away from Him.[72] This Fall came after eons of harmonious life in Heaven by its countless created inhabitants. By choosing to follow the Light Bearer (Lucifer) over the designated King of Heaven (Jesus), one-third of individual souls were cast into Hell (Revelation 12:3-4). J. Trigg explains Origen's teaching that the fallen souls had earned their dishonor.

From the Platonists also Origen takes the concept of preexistence of souls as a way to explain apparent injustice in the way providence operates. Thus Origen explained the distinction between souls who are vessels of honor and those who are vessels of dishonor in Romans 9, not on the basis of unmerited election, but on the basis of those souls' behavior before they were conceived in the womb. (PA 3.1.21)[73]

Each individual fallen soul slowly relearns its original divinity through multiple incarnations.

Point 2: "If anyone says or thinks that the soul of the Lord pre-existed and was united with God the Word before the Incarnation and Conception of the Virgin, let him be anathema."

Contra-Origen: From the Catechism of the Catholic Church:

The Father's only Son, conceived as man in the womb of the Virgin Mary, is "Christ", that is to say, anointed by the Holy Spirit, from the beginning of his human existence, though the manifestation of this fact takes place only progressively: to the shepherds, to the magi, to John the Baptist, to the disciples. (Cf. Mt 1:20; 2:1–12; Lk 1:35; 2:8–20; Jn 1:31-34; 2:11) Thus the

---

[71] Steenberg, "Origen and the Final Restoration."
[72] First Principles 2.8.3 and Ezek. 36:25–28.
[73] J. W. Trigg, *Origen* (London: Routledge, 1998), 28–29.

whole life of Jesus Christ will make manifest "how God anointed Jesus of Nazareth with the Holy Spirit and with power." (Acts 10:38)

Pro-Origen: Origen recognized in Yahweh ("I am who I prove myself to be") the Word of God, His Wisdom and His Truth. In First Principles Origen writes:

[F]or it is written, "The head of Christ is God;" seeing clearly also that it is written, "No one knoweth the Father, save the Son, nor doth any one know the Son, save the Father" (for who can know what wisdom is, save He who called it into being? or, who can understand clearly what truth is, save the Father of truth? who can investigate with certainty the universal nature of His Word, and of God Himself, which nature proceeds from God, except God alone, with whom the Word was), we ought to regard it as certain that this Word, or Reason (if it is to be so termed), this Wisdom, this Truth, is known to no other than the Father only.[74]

He acknowledged Jesus as the incarnation of the Word; the Son of God who was with God since the beginning of the Divine Creation (John 1:1). He existed before the world was created, before Abraham (John 8:58) and before John the Baptist (John 1:15). His mission on earth was to conquer death and to open up the gates of Heaven for the eventual return of all his divine subjects.

Point 3: "If anyone says or thinks that the body of our Lord Jesus Christ was first formed in the womb of the holy Virgin and that afterwards there was united with it God the Word and the pre-existing soul, let him be anathema."

Contra-Origen: It was during the Immaculate Conception that the Son of God was placed in the womb of the Virgin Mary, the "Mother of God" (Luke 1:28–35). As the church placed Jesus equal to God in all things at the Council of Nicaea, it follows that the birth of Jesus was a unique event

---

[74] First Principles 2.6.1.

in the history of mankind. We get the following explanation of the Catholic Church's teaching[75] of the birth of God in the form of Jesus:

Jesus is truly God, and is uniquely holy by reason of his divinity. Mary is human, and is holy by the grace and merits of her son. Jesus is free of original sin because he is God. Mary was kept free of original sin by the grace of Jesus. She was conceived by her parents in the normal way, but from the moment of her conception she existed in a state of union with God. She was granted the kind of grace and holiness which would have belonged to all human beings had there been no original sin.

It is also Catholic dogma that Mary remained free from personal sin throughout her life.... She was not immune to the problems of living in a world touched by sin. She had to cooperate with God's grace, and she had to cope with evil, above all the unjust murder of her son on the cross. Mary was tempted as we are. But she did not sin. She cooperated with God's grace, and in this she is a model for us. When we are tempted to think that sin cannot be defeated, Mary witnesses to the fact that the grace of Christ can conquer the powers of hell. Mary shows forth the goodness of God more than any other human being, except Jesus. Jesus is truly God, and is uniquely holy. Mary is the Mother of Jesus, and she is holy by the grace and merits of her Son and by her cooperation with God's grace.

Pro-Origen: Physically, Jesus was born in the way every child has ever been born, with the incarnated spirit body and its soul entering the fetus at birth. Jesus's human body was formed in the physical body of a virgin (spiritually pure) mother: Mary, the incarnated daughter of the Archangel Raphael.[76]

The materialistic concept of a virgin birth of Jesus is a consequence of the adaptation of the Trinity dogma by the church at the Council of Nicaea and was not part of Origen's theology. Benedikt Bauer investigates the claim that First Principles (Peri Archon) is the basis for the Trinity dogma in the church, and brings out the possibility that Origen's true theology (not

---

[75] From FAQ of the Virgin Mary http://www.amm.org/faq/Conception.aspx
[76] R. Sträuli, *Salomo der Königs Quelle* (ABZ Verlag Zürich, 1989).

that which it had been changed to) was a clear differentiation between the Father, the Son, and the Holy Spirit(s).

One of the most controversial treatises in Peri Archon can be found in I 3,5-8. The reason for this sensation is actually a fragment of Justinian, which is inserted here (in the German translation in, otherwise next to the text). Accordingly Origen said: "I believe that God the Father, who holds the universe together, penetrates to every being and gives each one out of his own (being) to be what it is. The son (works) less far than the father, who only penetrates to the creatures endowed with reason, for he is in second place after the father; still less far is the Holy Spirit, who only penetrates as far as the saints. To this extent, then, the power of the Father is greater than that of the Son and the Holy Spirit; greater then that of the Son than that of the Holy Spirit; and the efficacy of the Holy Spirit, for its part, surpasses that of all that is otherwise holy". As a consequence, this means a radical subordinatianism: Father, Son and Spirit are depotentingly subordinate to one another, and basically the transition from the Father to the creatures is fluid, because the difference between the Holy Spirit and "everything else that is holy", succinctly appears to be only a quantitative, not a qualitative step.[77]

When we take the statement of Jesus, "Believe me that I am in the Father, and the Father in me" (John 14:11), meaning that "His will is at one with God's will," and that the Holy Spirit(s) only support or speak through those who do God's will, we discover Origen teaching that they all do the will of God, but are subordinate as described.

Point 4: "If anyone says or thinks that God the Word has become like to all heavenly orders, so that for the cherubim he was a cherub, for the seraphim a seraph: in short, like all the superior powers, let him be anathema."

Contra-Origen: At the Council of Nicaea, God and the Word of God (Logos) were defined as one, a unity. Therefore, this belief is in direct conflict with

---

[77] B. Bauer, *Das ewige Werden in Gott und das zeitliche Werden der Welt* (Tactum Verlag Marburg, 1996), 43. Translated from Greman by Goodle.

the Creed of Nicaea as shown below and entitled to the judgment from that Council.

To exclude Arian error, the Council produced its own creed, which we call the Creed of Nicaea, to distinguish it from the Nicene Creed:

"We believe in one God, the Father, Almighty, maker of all things visible and invisible;

"And in one Lord Jesus Christ, the Son of God, begotten of the Father, only-begotten, that is, from the substance (ousia) of the Father; God from God, Light from Light, Very God from Very God, begotten not made, of one substance (homoousios, consubstantial) with the Father, through whom all things were made, both in heaven and on earth; who for us men and for our salvation came down and was incarnate, was made man, suffered, and rose again on the third day, ascended into heaven, and is coming to judge the living and the dead;

"And in the Holy Spirit."

And those who say: "There was a time when he was not", and: "Before he was begotten he was not", and: "He came into being from nothing", or those who pretend that the Son of God is "Of another substance (hypostasis), or essence (ousia)" [than the Father] or "created" or "alterable" or "mutable", the catholic and apostolic church places under a curse.[78]

Pro-Origen: Origen agrees that He is the only-begotten Son of God. But for Origen, the Logos is a separate reasonable being from God, who is the paradigm for all divine beings. Zwingli[79] notes in John 1:1 that "the Word is a divine being and not God."

Point 5: "If anyone says or thinks that, at the resurrection, human bodies will rise spherical in form and unlike our present form, let him be anathema."

---

[78] *The History of Christianity* (Oxford: Lion Publishing Plc, 1997), 166–167.
[79] Zürich Bibel.

Note: This English translation varies greatly from the meaning of the German, which reads as follows: "Wer behauptet oder glaubt, die Leiber der Auferstandenen seien [meist noch] 'gebeugte Gestalten', und wer nicht bekennt, dass wir als aufrechte [Gestalten] auferweckt werden – den treffe der Bannfluch!"

Contra-Origen: This is in conflict with the Apostles' Creed, which ends: "I believe in the Holy Spirit, the Holy catholic Church, the communion of saints, the forgiveness of sins, the resurrection of the body, and the life everlasting."

Pro-Origen: Origen's belief that the fallen spirit gradually returns to a perfect state through multiple earth lives was rejected by the council. The associated spiritual resurrections that occur after each person dies are mostly of spirits who have not yet been restored to their original divine purity. J. Daniélou provides an example of a soul at the beginning of its journey (Mary Magdalen) and one near the end its journey back to divinity (John) as Origen taught:

This is typical of Origen's method of interpretation. Places are figures of spiritual states. Going up and going down correspond to the soul's movements in the spiritual life. The different categories of people represent groups at different stages in the spiritual life. This might be due simply to the application of Christ's visible acts, as recorded in the Gospels, to the spiritual life, a perfectly legitimate proceeding. When Origen represents Christ's miracles of healing as figures of spiritual cures and takes Mary Magdalen at Jesus' feet as a figure of beginners and John resting on his breast as a figure of the perfect, his "contemplation" is in both instances quite justified and in John's case it is in the spirit of the text itself. But in the present passage something more than that is involved. The brothers of Jesus represent δυνάμεις. Downward movement is a figure of the Incarnation, in which, according to a theory familiar to Origen, the Word was accompanied by his brothers the angels, who came down with him. Consequently, the scene in the Gospels becomes a figure of this descent from heaven. The method is very close to Heracleon's, even though detached from the doctrine of the pleroma and applied to the doctrine of the Incarnation.[80]

---

[80] J. Daniélou, *Origen* (New York: Sheed and Ward, 1955), 192–193.

Point 6: "If anyone says that the heaven, the sun, the moon, the stars, and the waters that are above heavens, have souls, and are reasonable beings, let him be anathema."

Contra-Origen: Throughout the pagan cultures the celestial bodies have been recognized and worshipped as gods, therefore it is reasonable that this point be made by the church to stop those pagan activities and the worship of demons.

Pro-Origen: From Origen's spiritual view of the celestial bodies, he saw them as symbols of divine and fallen reasonable beings. Such symbolism has been prevalent throughout Greek literature. Compare Plato's use in Timaeus 41. Celestial symbolism is a thesis unto itself, but I will give a brief example of Origen's view. He regarded the sun as symbolizing Jesus—"I am the light of the world" (John 8:12)—and the moon as symbolizing Jesus's adversary, Lucifer (Cf. Job 25:5; Isaiah 1:13–15; 1 Corinthians 15:41). Therefore, the significance of the solar eclipse at the time of Jesus's death becomes apparent, symbolizing the short-lived victory of Lucifer, which momentarily extinguished the light of Jesus from this world. At the time of an eclipse, we all can see that the moon emits no light of its own, therefore at other times that the moon only partially reflects the light (Truth) of Jesus—the signature of the "master of lies."

Point 7: "If anyone says or thinks that Christ the Lord in a future time will be crucified for demons as he was for men, let him be anathema."

Note: Crouzel argues this idea of a double sacrifice came from a misunderstanding of Origen's teaching by Jerome.

In connection with the ritual scheme the cosmic and hypercosmic effect of the sacrifice of the Cross: as several texts show, He has purified everything, on earth as in heaven. That is why Origen speaks sometimes of a double efficacity of the one sacrifice. A similar affirmation in the Treatise on First Principles was understood in a wrong sense by Jerome: 'although Origen does not say so', Jerome nevertheless understands the matter as if Origen was affirming a duality of sacrifices, Christ having to be crucified again for the demons. But Book I of the Commentary on John of similar date to the Treatise on First Principles, clearly affirms the uniqueness of the sacrifice—'the victim once offered—ten hapax thysiam'—and at the same time its double efficacy. The uniqueness of the sacrifice is also affirmed in the Treatise on First Principles itself. Jerome must have misunderstood. He sees a confirmation of his point of view in the idea that Christ was made man among men, angel among angels, whence, as Jerome extends Origen's thought in his own way, we get demon among demons. But that Christ became a man among men and an angel among angels is only said in a very precise context, that of the theophanies, not that of Christ's sacrifice, and nothing justifies us in extending it to that.[81]

Contra-Origen: This is inconsistent with the doctrine of eternal damnation, supported by six references in the New Testament (Matthew 18:8, 25:41, 25:46; Mark 3:29; 2 Thessalonians 1:9; Jude 7).[82] Also, the Theodosian Code states:

We authorize the followers of this law to assume the title Catholic Christians; but as for the others, since in our judgment they are foolish madmen, we decree that they shall be branded with the ignominious name of heretics, and shall not presume to give their conventicles the name of churches. They will suffer in the first place the chastisement of divine condemnation and the second the punishment of our authority, in accordance with the will of heaven shall decide to inflict.[83]

Pro-Origen: Origen's teaching was actually that Jesus Christ came into this world to save all the lost (fallen) souls,[84] including those known to the church as demons, the princes of Heaven that fell into the deepest regions of Hell due to the considerable amount of guilt they had in helping bring about the Fall.

---

[81] Crouzel, *Origen*, 196–197.
[82] BibleHub.com, comment on 2 Thessalonians https://biblehub.com/commentaries/ellicott/2_thessalonians/1.htm
[83] Medieval Sourcebook: Banning of Other Religions, Theodosian Code XVI.i.2, http://www.fordham.edu/halsall/source/theodcodeXVI.html
[84] Compare First Principles 3.1.10.

For Origen, the Final Judgment occurred in the three days following Jesus's death on the cross. When He descended into Hell, after successfully passing all earthly tests, He conquered Lucifer and limited Lucifer's power over the inhabitants of earth, creating a new epoch. The last demon that Jesus's love will conquer will be Lucifer (Death). (Compare 1 Corinthians 15:20–28.) One example of the new epoch is distinguished in the disappearance of "possession by evil spirit." During the time of Christ, there are many documented cases of possession (df. Mark 1:27, 3:11, 5:2–13, 6:7, 7:25, 9:14–29; First Principles 3.2). After the final judgment on Lucifer, he and his evil spirits no longer have unlimited power over all the inhabitants of earth as they did at the time prior to Jesus's victory over him. In addition, he no longer can hold souls in Hell against their will, as was the case before Jesus opened Heaven's gate to all. (See discussion of demons in Origen's Commentary on the Gospel of John.)

Point 8: "If anyone says or thinks that the power of God is limited, and that he created as much as he was able to compass, let him be anathema."

Contra-Origen: M. C. Steenberg defends the view that the Almighty God can do anything (see also Luke 1:37):

Conversely, if God created the human soul in Adam, from which all other souls (except that of Christ) have been begotten, then God can surely exterminate anything He has created, or anything man has made, at any time He sovereignly chooses:—which, of course, is the principal theme of both Gen. 6:7 and Rev. 18.[85]

Pro-Origen: For the trusting mind, it may be a comforting thought that God's power is unlimited, but with deeper analysis this simple notion becomes illogical. With the benefit of the teachings of Plato, Euclid, Pythagoras, and Democritus, it was clear to Origen that God could not have created the Spiritual Laws and Natural Laws that He did, and simultaneously contradict those Laws. In this logical fashion, His own Laws must limit God's actions. This had a far deeper meaning for the priests and Pharisees, who had usurped God's power by becoming His

---

[85] Steenberg, "Origen and the Final Restoration."

voice on earth. They did not want their power limited in any fashion, but what resulted is a set of rules lacking logic and harmony with nature. From Origen's letter to Gregory we appreciate his suggested basis for understanding the scriptures.

And I would wish that you should take with you on the one hand those parts of the philosophy of the Greeks which are fit, as it were, to serve as general or preparatory studies for Christianity, and on the other hand so much of Geometry and Astronomy as may be helpful for the interpretation of the Holy Scriptures.[86]

Point 9: "If anyone says or thinks that the punishment of demons and of impious men is only temporary, and will one day have an end, and that a restoration (apokatastasis) will take place of demons and of impious men, let him be anathema."

From the Westminster Confession, chapter XXXII, we have the teaching about the wicked souls:

And the souls of the wicked are cast into hell, where they remain in torments and utter darkness, reserved to the judgement of the great day. (Luke 16:23, 24; Acts 1:25; Jude 6–7; 1 Pet. 3:19)

Edward Moore aptly defends Origen's restoration theory, summarizing:

The beauty of Origen's theory is that this truth is not forced upon us in a direct and violent manner, but is gradually revealed to us as an intelligible (or rational) as well as an existential verity.[87]

---

[86] Origen's letter to Gregory http://www.newadvent.org/fathers/1014.htm

[87] E. Moore, "Origen of Alexandria and apokatastasis", (Quodlibet, 2003), https://www.academia.edu/4958853/Origen_of_Alexandria_and_Apokatastasis.

The Verdicts from Today

Contra-Origen: From M. C. Steenberg we have this:

In the end, the doctrine of Universal Salvation cannot be faithfully paired with the more patristic notions of free will or final judgement, even though Origen energetically defends both; for he described "judgement" solely as a tool for teaching, and thus removed from it any real sense of justice. He exaggerated the love of God to a degree that downplayed His righteousness: two features which the Church has been insistent to bring together in its teachings, rather than to separate. Here we must admit a severe flaw in Origen's thought. Ultimately, his view of universal restoration took the concept of free will full-circle, and ended with its absence; for if all are indeed to be restored to God, then the "choices" one makes in life are really not choices at all—for the ultimate fruit of the decision is already determined by God.[88]

Pro-Origen: Those who have had the preparatory education prescribed by Origen can glimpse into his brilliance, understanding that his theology includes the truths from all religions while simultaneously illuminating the dogmas that have tainted them throughout history. By resisting the materialistic view of creation and by accepting a spiritual world, one is ready to hunt for the pearls within scripture (Matthew 7:6). It then becomes clear that the deeper meaning of the passages in Scripture (also Homer and Plato) deal with a spiritual world and its inhabitants that existed long before the physical world was created out of nothing thirteen billion years ago for the sole purpose of completely restoring the Divine Spiritual World. We, the fallen, will and have suffered separation from God for a material eternity, but this is only a short time for God and his divine children (2 Peter 3:8).

Heretic and Prophet

In looking at the books of the prophets a familiar pattern arises, that of the prophets being sent to teach the people of earth (the fallen souls) knowing in advance their divine message is not going to be widely accepted. In Ezekiel 3:7, God forewarns His prophet of the problems that he will encounter:

---

[88] Steenberg, "Origen and the Final Restoration."

"But the house of Israel will not hearken unto thee; for they will not hearken unto me: for all the houses of Israel are impudent and hardhearted." We consistently hear the prophets admonishing the earthly leaders for how they oppress and kill His people (those loyal to God). In Micah 3:1–3 we hear God's messenger speaking to all the worldly leaders, and the inquisitors: "And I said: Hear now, O heads of Jacob, and you rulers of the house of Israel: Is it not for you to know justice?"

Justice is a misconstrued word in the teachings of Jesus, especially today. It is commonly confused with retribution as distinct from the justice taught by Jesus, which calls for an entire repayment of all debts (Matthew 5:26) but allowing for all to be saved (Luke 15:4–7). Jesus, the Word, the King of God's heavenly creation, came to Earth to show us what divine Love is and to tell us what divine Justice means: "Love thy neighbor as thyself; turn the other cheek; not one shall be lost!" (see Matthew 19:19, 5:39; Luke 15:4). How can the "church" that violated these teachings of the Son of God by condemning millions to their death say Origen's humanistic theology is not the will of God?

God is especially speaking through Habakkuk to the likes of the Egyptians and Romans, who built their empires on massive bloodshed and inequitable class structures: "Woe to him who builds a town with bloodshed, who establishes a city by inequity!" (Habakkuk 2:12).

When we look at the life and work of Origen from the viewpoint of the prophets, it is conceivable to imagine him as being simultaneously a prophet of God and a heretic in the eyes of those admonished by the prophets, without any contradictions. What we know about Origen's method of writing, his volume of writing, and its precision clearly suggests divinity. His writings were dictated, and it took seven stenographers to keep up with him. He could speak logically and intelligibly on one biblical point for several hours without specific preparation. David G. Hunter says, "Origen's homilies were preached spontaneously, not prepared in writing."[89] These are all the characteristics of a prophet of God.

---

[89] David G. Hunter, "Origen's Writings", accessed June 3, 2021, https://www.copticchurch.net/patrology/schoolofalex2/chapter02.html.

In his letter to Africanus, Origen recounts missing references in the Hebrew text of the Bible describing the treachery of the scribes and Pharisees against the prophets, which he discovered in his work on the Hexapla, perhaps as a reminder to us about his own fate at the hands of the church:

At present, I shall adduce from the Gospel what Jesus Christ testifies concerning the prophets, together with a story which He refers to, but which is not found in the Old Testament, since in it also there is a scandal against unjust judges in Israel. The words of our Saviour run thus: "Woe unto you, scribes and Pharisees, hypocrites because ye build the tombs of the prophets, and garnish the sepulchres of the righteous, and say, If we had been in the days of our fathers, we would not have been partaken with them in the blood of the prophets. Wherefore be ye witnesses unto yourselves, that ye are the children of them which killed the prophets. Fill ye up then the measure of your fathers. Ye serpents, ye generation of vipers, how can ye escape the damnation of Gehenna? Wherefore, behold, I send unto you prophets, and wise men, and scribes; and some of them ye shall kill and crucify; and some of them shall ye scourge in your synagogues, and persecute them from city to city: that upon you may come all the righteous blood shed upon the earth, from the blood of righteous Abel unto the blood of Zacharias, son of Barachias, whom ye slew between the temple and the altar. Verily I say unto you, All these things shall come upon this generation." And what follows is of the same tenor: "O Jerusalem; Jerusalem, thou that killest the prophets, and stonest them which are sent unto thee, how often would I have gathered thy children together, even as a hen gathereth her chickens under her wings, and ye would not! Behold, your house is left unto you desolate."

Let us see now if in these cases we are not forced to the conclusion, that while the Saviour gives a true account of them, none of the Scriptures which could prove what He tells are to be found. For they who build the tombs of the prophets and garnish the sepulchres of the righteous, condemning the crimes their fathers committed against the righteous and the prophets, say, "If we had been in the days of our fathers, we would not have been partakers with them in the blood of the prophets." In the blood of what prophets, can any one tell me? For where do we find anything like this written of Esaias, or Jeremias, or any of the twelve, or Daniel? Then about Zacharias the son of Barachias, who was slain between the temple and the altar, we learn from Jesus only, not knowing it otherwise from any Scripture. Wherefore I think no other supposition is possible, than that they who had the reputation of wisdom, and the rulers and elders, took away from the people every passage which might bring them into discredit among the people. We need not wonder, then, if this history of the evil device of the licentious elders against Susanna is true, but was concealed and removed from the Scriptures by men themselves not very far removed from the counsel of these elders.[90]

We also find the motive of those being admonished to remove from history and the history books all that which shows their true character and their true motives.

Through this analysis I was unable to find unequivocal proof from the church that Origen's theology is false, on the contrary, I find greater support for Origen's theology through logic, reason, Ionian Greek philosophy, and the natural sciences. I, therefore, invite all those willing, to move past the debate over heresy until Origen's worldview is fully rediscovered. An open discussion from all viewpoints, in the tradition of Socrates, is needed to first understand Origen's theology and then investigate its impact on philosophy and the natural sciences.

---

[90] Origen's letter to Africanus http://www.newadvent.org/fathers/0414.htm

APPENDIX 3

The Gift of Reincarnation

PRIOR TO THE DAMNATION OF Origen, early Christians believed in reincarnation. But this was not the modern Hindu version of random endless reincarnation but rather one governed by the Laws laid down by Jesus (Yahweh). "Love thy neighbor as thyself" (Mark 12:31); "you must be perfect to enter into the Kingdom of God" (cf. Matthew 5:48); and "you will repay your debt to the last farthing" (cf. Matthew 5:26).

Under these Laws, reincarnation looks like this: Your spiritual body (created by God in His image prior to the Fall)[91] is placed into the newborn fetus by the Divine World. Locked in this material body, the spirit is in most cases unable to influence the heavy matter and surface into consciousness but serves as our subconscious, our true heart, our conscience, and our inner voice. The goal of this incarnation is to pay back the debt incurred in the Fall and to pay back the debt incurred in previous lives on earth, without being consciously burdened with the knowledge of past failures. The angels of God select the appropriate family and living conditions in which you are to grow up that will best provide the tests needed, accomplishing the goals set out for this life. Every virtue can be learned under the appropriate circumstances: patience, love, humility; generosity, forgiveness, and selflessness.

With this belief, the early Christians did not fear their oppressors. They knew that their next life on earth would be determined by how they felt and acted under the hand of their oppressors. They knew that God would provide the perfect penitence for their oppressors in their next life on earth and that they would not have worried about revenge. Their oppressors

---

[91] From Genesis 1:27 we have "So God created man in his own image, in the image of God he created him," and from John 4:23 "God is spirit, and his worshipers must worship in spirit and in truth." So Genesis should read: "So God created man's spirit in his own image ...."

would be born into conditions that would place them at the mercy of their fellow man, and they would likely suffer the same type of oppression that they had once practiced. This is what was meant by "an eye for an eye" (Exodus 21:24), but the early Christians knew that God was the only perfect Judge to administer this type of justice.

More important, for the would-be emperors of the world, people with this belief could not be controlled. They could not be forced to do things against their will or against the teachings of Jesus. They would live by their morals under any conditions of oppression and could not be forced to fulfill every wish of the emperor. People with this belief would avoid doing anything that would increase either their guilt or their fellow man.

This is why the emperor Justinian recognized Origen as such a serious threat to his empire and that the best way to gain control over the people was to strike fear into them. Control was gained by usurping God's authority as judge on earth and by creating the threat of eternal damnation. This threat was powerful to anyone who did not believe in reincarnation, and they could be persuaded to follow any dogma created by the church for the benefit of the emperor. But by declaring it also illegal to believe in the preexistence of the soul, he took away the meaning of life for humanity, and without meaning, it was easy to waste life. The church wasted lives for centuries, and modern Christians continue to waste them in the name of God.

It was by a narrow margin at the Fifth Ecumenical Council in AD 553 that the (physical) church eliminated the (spiritual) reincarnation teaching that had existed in the early Christian teachings of Jesus, Paul, John, and Origen. It is true that in His brief three years of teaching, Jesus did not specifically teach reincarnation. This was not His mission, which was rather to make sure that people believed He was the Son of God: our Savior and the King of Heaven. It is important to note He never denied reincarnation in his teachings, but He did acknowledge it a few times (see below). Jesus promised to send the Spirit of Truth (John 14:26) to teach the many spiritual teachings that Jesus did not have time to explain in detail and which the people of that time could not yet comprehend.

The Bible available to us today does not explain reincarnation in great detail, but there are numerous clear references to it. Looking at the many passages surrounding the second coming of Elijah (Malachi 4:5; Matthew 16:13–14, 17:10–13; Mark 6:14–16, 9:11–13; John 1:19–21), one gets the impression that reincarnation was a common belief at the time the Bible was written from all these comments about someone being born again and the longing for a prophet to come again. This would explain why there is not much detail on it, since one need not elaborate on understandings that are commonly held.

Nicodemus was concerned about his ability to change at such a late stage in his life when he asked Jesus: "How can a man be born when he is old? Can he enter a second time into his mother's womb and be born?" Jesus's answer was: "Most assuredly." In John 3:1–-21, Jesus is telling an elderly man, who had perfectly heard the teachings of Jesus, that clearly he did not have enough years left to change his ways, but that through God's love he would have at least another life in which he could live according to these new teachings.

Modern genetic research confirms it was impossible for any human to live to the ages quoted in the Old Testament. Genetic research done on human remains confirms there has been no change in the human body over this time period. Genesis 5:5 says: "So all the days that Adam lived were nine hundred and thirty years; and he died." This is not the same as saying Adam lived to be 930 years old. Saying that his total years on earth were 930 reconciles modern scientific knowledge with the Bible. It also helps properly place biblical events into both geological and archeological history, since Adam's 930 years could have been spread over a ten- to twenty-thousand-year span.

The eruption of the volcano Santorini (on the island of Thera, north of Crete) in 1646 BC has helped historians accurately date Joseph's life. The volcanic ash fallout from this eruption likely caused the seven years of famine foreseen by the Pharaoh, which forced Jacob and his family to travel[92] south to Egypt. With this, Jacob-Israel died around 1627 BC.

---

[92] R. Sträuli, "Wann wurde Josef nach Ägypten verschleppt?" (*Museion*, 2000, 1/1993).

Concurrently, archeologists have placed Abram's life in the twenty-second century BC. It does not take superhuman life spans to explain the missing four hundred years in this family history when you consider the possibility of multiple lives. Intuitively, it is hard to believe that the same Jacob who so easily stole his older brother's firstborn inheritance later patiently put up with many years of abuse to win the daughter of Laban. It is also hard to believe that the renowned hunter Esau let his brother get away with such a dirty trick. It is more likely that he tracked down and killed Jacob for his treachery shortly after he discovered it. This means the Jacob-Israel who woke up in Genesis 28:18 did so four hundred years later, in a new life on earth, and with a stronger belief in God. This logically explains Jacob's 147 years on earth, after dying in his eighties in Egypt. It also helps explain how Esau's family got so massive in what was earlier thought to have been a short period.

Reincarnation has widely been discussed in esoteric circles, but the modern medical community does not consider it as a serious possibility. Although scientific evidence exists, there is no concrete proof of multiple lives. But what if this is merely one of God's Laws? Life would no longer be a test if everyone knew they could keep trying until they finally got it right. Where would the need for belief go? Doesn't it require infinite love to allow a terrorist to enter a new life with a chance to correct his atrocious wrongdoings and not be plagued with the conscious memory of them? Such subconscious memories of past lives helps better explain the range of psychosis diagnosed in the youngest of children than modern medicine currently can.

A recent reanalysis of behavioral data collected on identical twins throughout the year can shed light on this subject. The current two-factor behavior model does not explain the data collected in identical twin studies. It includes only genetic and environmental factors as determinants of behavior. In other words, all behavior is determined solely by what you physically inherit from your parents and how you were raised. In the special case of identical twins, one of the two factors is thrown out since the physical inheritance is truly identical. Thus, the current model says the differences in behavior between two identical twins are solely due to how they were raised. Ask any mother of identical twins, and you will find that she cannot explain the behavioral differences of the two because she has painstakingly made sure that neither is favored. The statistical patterns observed in twin studies on alcoholism, smoking, criminal behavior, schizophrenia, attention deficit hyperactivity disorder, and bipolar disorder confirms her feeling, and they show there are other factors at play than are currently recognized by the medical profession. One of these factors is that each of us carries a certain amount of spiritual baggage or gifts into our lives.

Seeing the bigger picture, it is much easier to recognize the beauty of God's creation and to realize it is not He who is behind the evil in our world. Evil is clearly caused by our misuse of the free will that He gave to us. When we chose to follow Lucifer eons ago, we chose to reject Jesus's God-given right as the King of Heaven, and we were thrown out of Heaven along with Lucifer into the darkness and death (separation from God) of Hell. But fortunately for us, Jesus descended into Hell and broke Lucifer's tightfisted reign over us, and now we are free to return to Heaven. It is a long road, but once we have again accepted Jesus as our only King and rejected the "king of this world" (cf. John 13:36), we have unlimited support on our road to perfection from the Divine Spiritual World. People are placed in our path to help us; situations are created for us to learn and to repay our many debts; they will need to be repaid to the last farthing.

Physical human suffering is only His way of effecting meaningful spiritual teaching. By taking away the conscious knowledge of God and His love, God can test the true orientation of the spirit. Jesus had to pass this ultimate test Himself and to prove to Lucifer that He did maintain a true love to His Father regardless of all the tests that Lucifer put Him through during his physical life. Only after passing this ultimate test was Jesus able to descend into Hell with Michael and his army and to pass Final Judgment on Lucifer and the fallen (cf. Revelation 12:3–4, 7–9, 20:1–3). From St. Fulbert of Chartres (d. 1028) we have a poetic rendition of this occurrence.

> For Judah's Lion bursts his chains, crushing the serpent's head; and cries aloud through death's domains to wake the imprisoned dead.

Devouring depths of hell their prey at his command restore; his ransomed hosts pursue their way where Jesus goes before.

Reincarnation is the norm, divine incarnation is the exception, and demonic incarnation was limited to the time prior to the Final Judgment. The goal of reincarnation is restoration, the return of all the fallen to Heaven. Reincarnation is the greatest gift given to us by God. No matter how many times we fail, He will give us another chance to reach the required perfection so that we all can reenter His Kingdom. "Not one will be forgotten" (cf. Luke 12:4–7; John 18:8–9).

APPENDIX 4
A Return to the High Ethic of the Ionian Ideal

Why Return to the Ionian[iii] Greek Culture?

IT TOOK NEARLY TWO THOUSAND years[iv] for the physical sciences to return to the level of knowledge of the physical world known to the Ionians, recovering from the suppression that started with Sparta and ended with the Roman Catholic Church.[v] Modern philosophy has yet to achieve the broad reach that it possessed within the Ionian culture.[vi] This is seen in the modern definition of the word philosophy,[93] which specifically excludes bodies of knowledge that the Ionian philosophy (Ideal) harmoniously included. There was no body of knowledge that was and is not logically explained within the Ionian philosophy, which they defined as the love of wisdom (*philos* – friend and *sophia* – wisdom).

Especially in an age with both nuclear weapons and gene manipulation, such an all-encompassing ideal embraced by government, the scientific community, the business community, and the general population is desperately needed. The Ionian Ideal motivates people to pursue a virtuous life in lieu of an unscrupulous one. It provides the needed logical and reasonable explanation that only the highest ethical stand is acceptable.

---

[93] Philosophy: 1. the branch of knowledge or academic study devoted to the systematic examination of basic concepts such as truth, existence, reality, causality, and freedom; 2. a particular system of thought or doctrine; 3. a set of basic principles or concepts underlying a particular sphere of knowledge; 4. a precept, or set of precepts, beliefs, principles, or aims, underlying somebody's practice or conduct; 5.restraint, resignation, or calmness and rationality in a person's behavior or response to events; 6.the branch of learning that includes the liberal arts and sciences and excludes medicine, law, and theology (archaic). (Encarta World English Dictionary © 1999 Microsoft Corporation.)

The strides made in the last four hundred years in the physical sciences are fantastic.[vii] After having been freed from the control of the church, science has been able to help us understand the "how?" of our world. But a highly developed philosophy is required to complement this growing scientific knowledge to present a meaningful "why?" to mankind. Starting from the newly discovered understanding of the Ionian culture[viii] can help us form the basis of a philosophy worthy of explaining the great discoveries of science and bringing their meaning into the larger picture of our world.

Let us look at one example where a greater understanding is desperately needed today. A pure mathematical view of the identical twin studies done throughout the last decades has shown that at least five independent variables are required to define the statistical variances found in human behavior and chronic disease.[ix] Modern medicine only recognizes two of these five required variables: genetics and environment. Insufficient understanding and acceptance of the missing three factors is responsible for modern medicine's insufficient successful treatment of emotional and mental disorders, as well as chronic disease. This was not the case in the Ionian culture because their philosophy helped them understand the three other "soft" factors currently overlooked by modern medicine.[94]

The benefits this ideal brings are many, but I have merely listed a few.

+ Creates a framework for understanding both current and historical events.
+ Improves the interpersonal environments in the workplace, at home, and in the community.
+ Broadens the understanding of sickness, poverty, and personal suffering.
+ Brings reason and logic back to areas where personal interpretation and dogma have reigned for centuries.
+ Builds the needed bridges between science, daily experience, and belief.

---

[94] Edward Bach, Heal Thyself: an Explanation of the Real Cause and Cure of Disease (C. W. Daniel, 1966).

Rediscovering Socrates

As with many great figures of history, a true understanding of Socrates has faded over time. Recent researchers have carefully applied the scientific method to present numerous of these important figures in a new light: their contemporaries.[x] The pictures that emerge are exciting and present our society with perfect role models.

Socrates placed his highest value on teaching people to use their reason in all walks of life. Only through reason can man come to higher knowledge and ethics. He spent his life seeking goodness, truth, and beauty while remaining true to his virtues of modesty and self-knowledge. One can imagine, with these noble requirements for the true philosophy, how philosophy became fragmented over time. Understanding the true philosophy requires strict pursuit of the highest ethical standard.

For many years, Plato's dialogues were presumed to have been fictitious, but they were not. A better understanding[95] of the Ionian culture has shown us how professional journalists of the time were motivated to stenograph[xi] the discussions of the best-known personalities. This allowed him the greatest possible circulation for the published work. Plato's motivations were nobler,

---

[95] *Museion* 2000, 3/1999, 39

but his tactics were the same. He wanted to thank his teacher of thirty years by making sure that Socrates's words and lessons lived on.

Knowing now that real people were involved in the dialogue, it is possible to achieve considerable insight into the various philosophical differences that existed within the Greek culture. It is also impressive to see Socrates in action as a teacher. He was too modest and too wise to stand up and preach his ideas to others. Rather, he used his wisdom, reason, and humor to help his opponent discover the truth for himself. He did this by asking thought-provoking, exacting questions and accepting only exact answers.

Today, people tend to view the Greeks as one people and do not recognize the internal struggle that continually existed between the Ionians and the Dorians.[96] But Socrates knew exactly who belonged to which camp. In Plato's dialogues, he allows both the Ionians and the Dorians to fully express their opinions, allowing the reader to realize the inherent differences in the two groups' views of the world. Below is a list of the typical traits of these two opposing ends of the Greek culture.

Ionian[xii]	Dorian[xiii]
Settlers	Conquerors
Builders	Takers
Democracy	Monarchy (Tyranny)
Wisdom	Power
Love	Lust
Spiritual (Music, Art, Poetry)	Material (Temples, Graves)
Freedom	Slavery
Reason	Mystery
Truth	Dogma
Sexual Equality	Male-Dominance
Respect	Sarcasm

---

[96] Dorians: A Greek people who took their name from Dorus, son of Hellen. They came from north or northwest and invaded Corinth, then Crete in 1100 BC; Spartans always regarded as representatives of unmixed Dorian ancestry. (From Compton's Interactive Encyclopedia Deluxe © 1999 The Learning Company, Inc.)

Highlights of the Ionian Ideal

+ No contradictions between any subjects across the entire educational spectrum.
+ Longing for the wisdom of Eros and the love of Zeus.[xiv] (Socrates treasured the spirit of the youth while Pausanias[97] lusted after the young body.)
+ A society built on the concept of a true democracy where the good of the whole can only be achieved through the good of individual, where each member has a set of responsibilities that are fully appreciated by the remaining members.[xv]
+ The fine arts carry with them the greatest social demands. They have the requirement to help guide mankind to the highest ethical standard. If it does not have this goal, by the Ionian definition, it is not art.
+ Great care taken in teaching the young minds. They fully understood the importance of providing children with a well-balanced and logical social structure[xvi] in which to learn. They followed the well-proven rule of never teaching a child something known to be false.[xvii] The example given to us by Socrates and Maria Montessori must be followed in all areas.
+ Works (whether they be theories, art, music or laws) created within the Ionian Ideal have passed the test of time.
+ More than three thousand years later, Homer's poems are still the most inspiring ever written.
+ Modern researchers[xviii] continually go back to the works of Euclid, Pythagoras, and Plato in order to help interpret the latest scientific discoveries.
+ Galileo and Einstein have drawn on it in recent history in order to develop their laws and theories.
+ Works created outside of this Ideal have not passed the test of time.
+ The definition of the word *philosophy* needed to change throughout the years in order to justify Aristotle's imperfect view of the world.

---

[97] Pausanias was a Dorian aristocrat from Athens who lived at the time of Socrates. See Plato's Symposium.

Only those areas of his philosophy that he learned from Plato have passed the test of time.

+ Just as Friedman incorrectly defined the free market, Darwinism does not fully explain the beauty, the diversity, and the many symbioses in nature.

+ The modern model for human behavior and disease fails to recognize more than half of the responsible factors.

+ American universities admit that their current curriculum can only supply 20 percent of what is needed for their graduates to be successful in life.[98]

+ The deterministic mechanics founded by Galileo and enhanced by Newton appears to break down at the atomic level. Against the recommendation of Einstein, a probabilistic approach to quantum mechanics was adopted, avoiding the consequences of a deterministic model.[xix]

"There is no one to whom history has nothing important to teach."[99]

A broad adaptation of the Ionian Ideal will put an end to the monotonous repetition of social and humanitarian disasters and show that the best route for mankind is to pursue only the highest ethic. By using the systematic methods given to us by Socrates and Galileo, we need to examine history. Only by understanding a person's philosophy and their personal motives are we able to determine whether our children should be given them as personal idols or as negative examples. The current nonjudgmental view toward historical figures leaves open the opportunity for every generation to pursue these same negative virtues with materialistic short-term rewards. We must show our children, in a logical and reasonable form, how the behavior of various historical individuals has impacted mankind, both positively[xx] and negatively[xxi]—not only showing them how much a single individual can contribute to society, but also giving them the needed tools to interpret their current environment and to make their own impact.

---

[98] Daniel Goleman, *Emotional Intelligence* (Bantam Books, 1997).
[99] From Friedrich Schiller's exceptional academic speech at the University of Jena on 26 May 1789.

A Framework for the Study of History

More than 250 years ago, Sir William Jones discovered the relationship between the Indo-European languages that led to the linguistic hypothesis that all peoples of Europe originated from Mesopotamia. It was not until recently that genetic researchers confirmed this hypothesis, which framed the bold assertion that modern man descended from Mesopotamia.

When looking at the early history of this area, a clear picture emerges of two distinct types of societies: those who settled and cultivated the land (Celts) and those who conquered it (Caucasians). The characteristics of these two types of peoples were described above, and the roots of all peoples can be traced back to these two basic and distinctive lifestyles and philosophies. When looking back into history, it is the ancestors of the Celts that are hardest to find because their societies did not leave behind many monuments, certainly none as momentous as could have been built with slave labor.

When looking at history, it is important to understand which philosophy one is studying. The following points need to be considered.

+ First of all, answer the following questions: How did they treat their own people, their neighbors, and their enemies?[xxii] (Switzerland has been a democracy, and without war, for over seven hundred years! They have never had slavery or taken land from their neighboring countries, and they accept equally all four ethnic constituents of their population.)
+ Use the modern understanding of human rights to judge the societies of the past and their people. Those who fulfill our modern understanding are possible role models to follow; those who don't are example to learn from.
+ Understand why a culture or society was really destroyed or conquered. What threat did it pose, or what profit did it present to the captor? Why did those books need to be burned or retranslated?[xxiii] Socrates shows us that the pursuit of the truth can only be good and that falsehoods are easily revealed through logic and reason. So how can books ever be bad?

+ Do not be blinded by great, materialist achievements. Understand how these were achieved and what "higher" goal they served.[xxiv]
+ Look for traces of the conquered culture in the slave labor that they may have been forced to perform. (Ionian Greek slaves performed nearly all of the fine art, medicine, and construction in Rome.)

Requirements for achieving the Ionian Ideal

Only by fulfilling all the following is it able to re-achieve the high level of understanding of all areas of study and life.

+ A complete scientific understanding – One that explains not only "how's" of the physical world but attempts to answer the "why's" of our entire world.
+ A schooled reason – In conjunction with the use of reason in every aspect of life, an exact thinking is also a requirement. Socrates said that mathematical studies help us to find the pure reason.[100]
+ The use of the scientific method in all areas of study, not just science.
+ High ethical standards and pursuit of virtues – For Socrates and Plato, a high ethical standard played a central role in their scientific and philosophical research.[101]

In Origen's[xxv] Peri Archon, he recommends starting with an observation of nature to form a basis for all areas of research. He particularly recommended that everyone use logic and reason to understand the vast differences in character, fate, and even body structure between individuals and groups.

It would be a worthy goal for a school to attempt to provide its students with a framework in which they can understand and analyze every situation that awaits them in life. It may be too much to ask that all children achieve this goal, but it would be infinitely satisfying to witness one child approach the level reached by Socrates or Plato.

---

[100] Plato, The Republic, 521–541.
[101] Plato, The Republic, 485.

APPENDIX 5
We All Have the Same Spiritual Ancestry

GOD GAVE MOSES THREE DIVINE gifts during his forty days on Mount Sinai. The first one, the Ten Commandments, has formed the basis for social justice throughout the world. We take them for granted today, but they were given to Moses at a time when no social law existed.

Only the Jews recognize the second gift, although they lost its true meaning during their Babylonian exile (597 to 538 BC). The Menorah has become a symbol of Judaism, but it was originally much more than that.

The third gift has only been recognized recently, and to many people today, appears to be a minor gift. On Friday, April 27, 1244 BC, Moses led the Israelites out of Egypt. At this point in history the only form of written communication available was picture based. These types of languages have numerous pictures. Egyptian hieroglyphics have had over ten thousand pictures through the course of their history. Those able to learn to read and write hieroglyphics were only the most highly educated. Fortunately, Moses grew up in the house of the Pharaoh and received this type of education. It would prove to be a tremendous asset when it came time for him to learn the new alphabet that God would give him on Mount Sinai.

The forty days that Moses spent with God on the Mount would be a conceivable length of time in which a person who could read and write a picture-based language could learn a twenty-four-character alphabet and write the Ten Commandments onto some flat stones in this new alphabet. If God had merely conjured them up out of the rocks, Moses would not have needed to be away from his people for so long. It is likely that the Ten

Commandments were written in the hand of Moses, but since they have not been found, we presently cannot prove this theory.

The first signs of an alphabet-based writing discovered by archeologists have been dated to 1231 BC. These were found in the Sinai desert, and the dating fits within the forty years that the Israelites spent there. Since then, many cultures adopted this ingenious, simple form of communication. It has allowed every man, woman, and child the opportunity to read and correspond, regardless of the house they grew up in.

Now that we understand the overwhelming social and spiritual value of both the first and third gifts from God, let us return to the second gift. It cannot be possible that God was just telling Moses how to build an attractive, decorative lamp for the temple. It must have a similar spiritual or symbolic value as the other two gifts.

The description of the Menorah in Exodus 25:31–40 does not give any initial hint to its true meaning. Physically, it can still be seen today in Rome. It is engraved in the Arch of Titus, depicting the Romans bringing back the spoils from their victory over the Jews in AD 70. It has a substantial base with a single column in the center that supports the six arms. Everything is symmetrical about the center column. In total there are seven places for lights and twenty-four knobs in total on the six arms.

What could the seven lights and twenty-four knobs symbolize? Besides the twenty-four-character alphabet mentioned above, where else in the Bible do we come across twenty-four? The most obvious is the twenty-four elders that John describes after God allowed him to open his spiritual eyes and glance into Heaven (Revelation 4:1–11). John also describes the seven lights at the top of the Menorah as the seven Spirits of God before the throne of God.

If we look at the Menorah as being symmetric about the center column, then we realize that these twenty-four knobs could also symbolize twelve pairs. This means they could symbolize the twelve tribes of Israel. The seven lights at the top then become three pairs plus one that stands alone. This one is on top of the column that supports all, the six plus the twenty-four. Is it the trunk of a spiritual family tree? Jesus/Yahweh often depicted Himself in this role. For instance, He called Himself the vine and us its branches. The other six lights would then symbolize the six archangels.

When we look further at John's descriptions of the throne, we recognize there are "four living creatures" between the twenty-four elders and the throne. This is likely his description of the symbolism associated with these three plus the one. When we compare John's four creatures with the gods of Egypt, we find considerable similarity. I mentioned in my last article, the three gods of Egypt—Amon (Lucifer), Horus (Aholah), and Hathor (Aholibah)—carry the symbols of lion/sphinx, falcon, and cow respectively. When we add Maat to these three, we get the same picture as John describes, since Maat is always depicted in Egypt with a human face.

The common opinion of Revelation is that God was showing John what was to come. But when we realize John's revelation was one looking back in time, before the Fall, things become clearer. This allows us to match the three fallen archangels up with their Heavenly counterparts: Raphael with Lucifer as lioness and lion, Gabriel and Aholah as eagle and falcon, and Michael and Aholibah as steer and cow.

In the description of paradise in Genesis, we find "the river Pishon skirts the whole land of Havilah." The river Pishon is symbolic for Jesus/Yahweh, and the three features found in the land of Havilah are good: gold (yellow), bdellium (white), and onyx (black). After the Fall, when Lucifer was now referred to as "the tree of the knowledge of good and evil," Jesus/Yahweh had only three of the Archangels with Him: Gabriel, Raphael, and Michael.

There is one other notable twenty-four, and each of us carries it with us: our twelve pair of ribs. Since we know that Eve was created from a rib, it would be worthwhile to consider this symbolic relationship. Our ribs differ from the Menorah in one respect: all twenty-four knobs are attached to the center column in the Menorah, but only fourteen ribs are attached to the sternum. We have fourteen true ribs and ten false ribs that are not connected to the sternum. We know that one-third of Heaven fell with Lucifer in the Fall. It could, therefore, be that fourteen of the twenty-four elders remained true to Jesus/Yahweh (the sternum), and the other ten fell along with Lucifer and the other two lesser-known archangels. Therefore, Eve was not created from just a rib; she was created from a false rib. This concept is supported by the depiction in the Bible of the beast with ten horns (Lucifer with the ten elder followers) in Daniel 7:17–24 and Revelation 17:1–12.

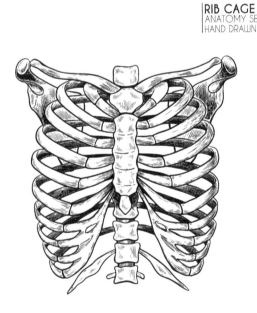

RIB CAGE
ANATOMY SET
HAND DRAWN

God's second gift to Moses, the Menorah, is not merely a pleasant table decoration; it is a spiritual family tree. It symbolizes Jesus/Yahweh, the only-begotten Son of God, through whom all of us were created. It shows the three houses of Heaven, as they originally were, all stemming from Jesus/Yahweh, Raphael, and Lucifer, founders of the white race; Aholah and Gabriel, leaders of the yellow race; and Aholibah and Michael heading the black race. All God's creation is one big family, and every part of His family was torn apart in the Fall. All of us, regardless of race, have suffered equally from the Fall. All of us are on the same road back to God; it is just that some of us have only started the journey while others are lucky enough to be close to the final goal. Someone's race cannot declare how far down the road they are; it only declares to the world the tremendous diversity in God's creation.

APPENDIX 6
Exploring Holistic Dimensions

*Develop the multi-faceted gifts of each child to unleash
their full spectrum of human potential
By: Anjum Babukhan*

"Your children are not your children.
They are sons and daughters of Life's longing for itself.
They come through you but not from you.
And though they are with you yet they belong not to you.
You may give them your love but not your thoughts,
For they have their own thoughts.
You may house their bodies but not their souls,
For their souls dwell in the house of tomorrow, which
you cannot visit, not even in your dreams.
You may strive to be like them, but seek not to make
them like you.
For life goes not backward nor tarries with yesterday.
You are the bows from which your children as living
arrows are sent forth.
The archer sees the make upon the path of the infinite,
and He bends you with His might that His arrows may
go swift and far.
Let your bending in the archer's hand be for gladness.
For even as He loves the arrow that flies, so He also loves
the bow that is stable." —Khalil Gibran[102]

THE CYCLE OF BIRTH AND death is part and parcel of life. We all come
from the same Divine Intelligence and children appear to have a natural

---

[102] Kahlil Gibran, *The Prophet*, (Penguin Classics, 2019)

connection to the Source. Parental and societal conditioning sometimes eclipse this inherent connection with the passage of time. To quote Fred Rogers, "as human beings, our job in life is to help people realize how rare and valuable each one of us really is." Children are naturally curious, creative and constantly ask questions. Ken Robinson in his famous ted talk questioned, "Are schools killing creativity?" Children's natural propensities and abilities can be further nourished and channelized in children as they are required for the 21st century.

"It is easier to build strong children than to repair broken men," quoted Frederick Douglass. This is a profound truth that foundational resilience can propel children to be prepared for any challenge they may face in the world. Neuroplasticity inherent in our dynamic brains allows us to continue to learn throughout our lifetime. However, the early childhood years have been identified as the best time to cultivate the strength for the roots of their character that will flourish in their future.

One of the metaphors that has moved me greatly is the *Law of Harvest* which Stephen Covey talks about in his famous bestseller, *7 Habits of Highly Effective People*. The universal truth of, "what we sow, we reap" is found every major religion's scripture in some form or the other. A passage by Samuel Smiles is quoted by Covey that we have adopted into a school song, **"Sow a Thought, Reap an Action, Sow an Action, Reap a Habit, Sow a Habit, Reap a Character, Sow a Character, Reap a Destiny"** Human values such as empathy, gratitude, integrity and kindness are easy to nurture during the tender childhood years. Childhood is the best time to hard-wire holistic habits that unleash their potential across the body, mind, heart and spirit - into the deepest depths of the sub-conscious mind.

Whether at home or at school, one must ensure that all the stages of *Maslow's Hierarchy of Human Needs* are addressed in the foundational years. After the base requirement for one's *physiological needs* of food, water, shelter, one's needs to feel *safe* and protected. After feeling secure, children need to feel that they belong and are loved. After feeling cherished and valued, self-esteem and self-efficacy spring up and continue to grow. Receiving love, connection and *belongingness* leads to a healthy *self-esteem*.

A lack of healthy self-esteem in childhood can impact the ability to form deep relationships and connect to one's own self as an adult. If a child's self-esteem is not properly nurtured in the early years, it can lead to social-emotional challenges later in life. It is after all these levels of childhood, children are ready to learn and satisfy their *intellectual needs*. Subsequently, aspirations for the arts and *aesthetic needs* can be appreciated. Pursuing of *self-actualization or self-transcendence* is found at the top of the pyramid as the loftiest goal according to Maslow.

As George Bernard Shaw rightly said, "Life isn't about finding yourself. Life is about creating yourself." Self-efficacy and self-regulation play a huge role in creating your inner capacity to realizing the full potential of your being. Carol Dweck discerns that, *"Becoming* is better than *being."* While pursuing my Ed.M in Human Development and Psychology from Harvard, I came across a lot of research materials from developmental science that supported a program called **Whole Person Approach (WPA)** that I put together. It grew rather organically after my years of application of Covey's habits and Gardner's multiple intelligences by synergizing the two together across the social-emotional, physical, cognitive and spiritual dimensions. WPA as a program, was found to help children develop self-efficacy, growth mindset and self-regulation.

Walter Mischell had shown the beneficial effects of *self-regulation* and *delayed gratification* in his famous Stanford *Marshmallow Experiment* way back in 1972. Self-regulation is a very important skill that is a proven predictor of future success. According to the famous author of *Emotional Intelligence,* Daniel Goleman," ....goal directed self-imposed delay of gratification is perhaps the essence of emotional self-regulation: the ability to deny impulse in the service of a goal, whether it be building a business, solving an algebraic equation, or pursuing the Stanley Cup." Self-regulation can also be taught by nurturing habits that support it. As Stephen Covey shared, habits are an overlap of knowledge, skill and desire.

Proposed by the psychologist Albert Bandura, *self-efficacy* affects every area of human endeavour and determines the beliefs a person holds regarding their power, skill and agency to affect situations. It influences person's choices, willingness to accomplish tasks or face challenges competently. Educator Kathy Kolbe adds, "Belief in innate abilities means valuing one's particular set of cognitive strengths. It also involves determination and perseverance to overcome obstacles that would interfere with utilizing those innate abilities to achieve."

Growth mindset provides a fertile field for us to believe that our intelligence, creative abilities, and character are things that we can improve in meaningful ways. We can always learn and get better at what we do. Carol Dweck proposed that, "in a growth mindset, people believe that their most basic abilities can be developed through dedication and hard work—brains and talent are just the starting point. This view creates a love of learning and a resilience that is essential for great accomplishment (Dweck, 2015)."

To develop holistically means to address all the dimensions namely - Body, Mind, Heart and Spirit. In my 25 years in education, I have chosen an eclectic approach by grafting developmental psychology, neuroscience and the best of self-empowerment to bring together a beautiful combination of how children (or adults) can be nurtured across these holistic domains. As a student of human development and psychology, as well as a teacher trainer, I have been a fan and promoter of methodology based on Dr. Howard Gardner's Theory of Multiple Intelligence which defines eight different neural pathways to cognition and competency skill sets. MI are like multiple pathways for expressing oneself. Every child is gifted, only in different ways and we need to accept and embrace the uniqueness and give them the space and support to grow and evolve. In our schools, we coined the phrase, "the more ways you teach, the more children you reach." Moreover, I have found that the much needed 21st Century skills of Collaboration, Communication, Creativity, Critical Thinking and Character (this was a C added by me personally) overlap with the MI serendipitously. MI and 21st Century skills are parallel and entwined in linking developmental science to practice.

Studying self-empowerment literature, I have personally benefited a great deal from Dr. Stephen Covey's *7 Habits of Highly Effective People.* Our private education group is also a *Leader in Me (LIM) School* (K-12 application of 7 Habits). I believe the 7 Habits' principles propel human effectiveness from the inside-out and empower you to lead your own life before we can effectively lead others. It also encourages you to *sharpen the saw* to keep one cutting-edge in the holistic human evolution. The First Habit - **Be Proactive** speaks of tapping into the space between stimuli and response wherein lies our greatest freedom-the freedom to choose our response. This is an echo from Viktor Frankl's book, *Man's Search for Meaning*. Children must be taught such valuable and universal principles from a very young age so that the roots go deep down into the foundations of their character helping them to become strong well-grounded holistic beings.

As parents and educators, we have a great responsibility on our shoulders to tap into the innate potential of each child to help them become the best version of themselves. Helping our children cultivate a healthy growth mindset, self-efficacy and self-regulation will go a long way to support them as co-creators of their destiny. Giving them the support to accommodate their neurodiversity and creating a safe space for inclusion goes a very long way in helping them become holistic human beings.

Author Marianne Williamson quoted, "the thought system of the human race is dominated by fear and has been for ages. So enlightenment is an unlearning of the thought system based on fear and an acceptance instead of the thought system based on love. A miracle is a shift of perception from fear to love." Let us help our children to hold on to and operate from the mindset of love and abundance instead of operating from fear and scarcity. We can become role models offering what transformational leadership (Bass, 1993) coined the four I's – *Idealized Influence, Intrinsic Motivation, Intellectual Stimulation and Inspirational Motivation*. Idealized Influence requires us to be role models and walk our talk. Inspirational Motivation radiates a contagious energy from an unconditional heart space of love and abundance. Intellectual Stimulation and Intrinsic Motivation encourages children to be the best and most authentic versions of themselves. Being comfortable in your skin leads to acceptance of self. All these are key and unlock the door to self-realization. Let us nurture our children from the heart space and empower them to develop the full spectrum of their potential. I would like to end with this quote from the Dalai Lama, **"Give the ones you love wings to fly, roots to come back and reasons to stay."**

To Sum up:

* Often, we find that parents tend to push down their dreams and desires onto their children, not realizing that each child is uniquely gifted and must be given the space to evolve into the full spectrum of potential. The beautiful poem coined by Khalil Gibran sums up the ideal perspective from which a parent should view their child.
* In today's world, we see a lot of brokenness and mental health issues among the adults. This epidemic of depression and other mental disorders can be prevented by nurturing holistic personalities starting from the tender childhood years wherein it is easier to build a strong foundation of Character. This is aptly summed by Frederic Douglass where he says "it is easier to build strong children than to repair broken men."
* Theories like Maslow's Hierarchy of Needs, Multiple Intelligence, 21st century Skills, 7 Habits, WPA and Transformational Leadership's Four I's are all tools that we can leverage to help our children become the best version of themselves by developing self-efficacy, self-regulation, growth mindset and self-acceptance and encouraging a thought system based love and abundance.

  o Recognize and encourage the unique potential of each child
  o The need for Security, Love and Belongingness and Self-esteem precede intellectual Needs
  o Provide Multiple pathways for learning and expression. *The more ways we teach the more children we reach.*
  o Develop all dimensions namely: Body, Mind, Heart and Spirit
  o Empower your child by operating from your heart space and facilitating a shift in perception from fear to love and abundance. *"There is no person in the whole world like you. And I like you just the way you are."* **Fred Rogers**

REFERENCES

Bandura, A. (1977). Self-efficacy: Toward a unifying theory of behavioural change. Psychological Review, 84(2), 191–215. https://doi.org/10.1037/0033-295X.84.2.191

Bandura, A. (1986). Social foundations of thought and action: A social cognitive theory. Englewood Cliffs, NJ: Prentice-Hall.

Bandura, A. (1994). Social cognitive theory of mass communication. In J. Bryant & D. Zillmann (Eds.), LEA's communication series. Media effects: Advances in theory and research, 61–90. Lawrence Erlbaum Associates, Inc.

Bandura, A. (1997). Self-efficacy: The Exercise of Control. W.H. Freeman and Company, New York.

Covey, S. (2005). Law of harvest. https://resources.franklincovey.com/mkt-7hvl/law-of-the-harvest-2

Dweck, C. S.(2015). Growth. British Journal of Educational Psychology. The British Psychological Society, 85, 242-245. https://doi.org/10.1111/bjep.12072

Gibran, K. (1923). On Children. The Prophet. Alfred A. Knopf.

Goleman, D. (1995). Emotional Intelligence. Bantam Publishers.

Frankl, V. (2008). Man's Search for Meaning. RHUK (Exported Edition).

ENDNOTES

i Footnotes from the quoted sections of Origen's Commentary on the Epistle to the Romans:

1. See Introduction (7).
2. Cf. Epilogue of Rufinus (6).
3. Origen is often referred to as Adamantius, "Man of Steel" or "Man of Adamant"; cf. Eusebius, Ecclesiastical History 6.14.10 and Jerome, Ep 43. Euseius says that he was known by this name even during his lifetime and that the epithet denoted the firmness with which Origen stood like a rock against heretics. Jerome thought it signified Origen's unwearied industry in producing innumerable books.
4. Cf. Hom in en 9.1.
5. Interpolati sunt ipsi libri See Introduction (7). The only other appearance of interpolare in the Commentary occurs in 10-43.2, where it is used to describe Marcion's work of tampering with the Scriptures.
6. See Introduction (7).
7. See Preface to Rufinus (2)
8. Hammond, "Last Ten Years," p. 404, elucidates Rufinus's intentions in this passage: "Rufinus' stand against such plagiarism, which seemed more surprising to his contemporaries than it does to us, was an implied criticism of Jerome's methods in his biblical commentaries. The procedure that he refuses here … is similar to that for which he had attacked Jerome and those like him earlier. By directly translating Origen, he himself will reveal to Latin readers the source of Jerome's vaunted learning as a biblical commentator." For a detailed examination of Jerome's plagiarism of Origen's Pauline exegesis, see C. Bammel, "Origen's Pauline Prefaces," pp. 495–513, in *Origeniana Sexta: Origene et la Bible/Origen and the Bible*, ed. Gilles Dorival and Alain Le Boulluec (Leuven: Leuven University Press, 1995).

ii The Anathematisms of the Emperor Justinian against Origen (Labbe and Cossart, Concilia, Tom. v., col. 677.) It was issued in AD 543 but wasn't ratified into the church until the Fifth Ecumenical Council in Constantinople in 553, at which time additional points were added to the original nine.

iii The Goths and the Celts shared this ethic, but they did not leave the literary wealth of the Ionians.

iv It was common knowledge at the height of the Ionian culture (seventh to fifth century BC) that the earth is round and that the sun is at the center of the solar system, which was in conflict with the Aristotelian view adopted by the church seven hundred years after Aristotle's death.

v Galileo Galilei (1564–1642) founded the modern scientific method. In order to do so, he had to leave the university, which was teaching Aristotle's dogmatic view of the world, and go back to the teachings of Euclid and Archimedes. While being a devout believer, he was still brought before the "holy inquisition" for his rediscovery of the sun's central position in the solar system. His work was built on the foundations created by Nicolas Copernicus, after whom this revolution is named.

vi Through the writings of Plato, we are able to get a taste of the high ethical level reached by the likes of Socrates. His dialogues do not give the typical one-sided view, but rather he allows his enemies the ability to voice their entire opinion. They allow the deep-thinking reader the ability to see each speaker's true spirit.

vii Science has rapidly developed after the Dark Ages, but medical, emotional, spiritual, and ethical development has not kept pace.

viii The Ionian culture was a democracy built on equal rights for all. They valued the high virtues of modesty, generosity, patience, and charity, and their philosophy teaches the requirement for pursuing only them. Art and music were a part of everyday life, where the laws were sung to the people so that they went deep into their hearts.

ix Abstract of "Updated Model for Human Behavior": The current model used in research for all walks of medicine has only two independent factors: genetics and environment. This simple model breaks down quickly when looking at identical twin studies, especially the study of infant twins, since both variables are equal. We have been analyzing the data collected from various identical twin studies in order to find a more robust causality model for both nonhereditary disease and behavior in humans. The model that we are currently testing has three additional independent factors. These have been hypothesized in order to describe the pattern found in all behavioral research data. Nonhereditary disease occurrence data fits well into this more robust model, and study of this data may also bring with it a better understanding of a possible sixth factor needed to fully explain human behavior and disease.

x How can it be that people who, with no personal motives, provided a great service to mankind? A study of the case of Ludwig van Beethoven exemplifies the mechanism used to turn a truly great person into a highly questionable eccentric. But since we still have access to so much information about Beethoven, it is possible today for the careful researcher to rediscover the true genius and soul of the man who left mankind with his timeless works. Jeanne d'Arc is another such case, whose truly heroic efforts have been overshadowed by the personal opinions of individual writers. Taking a close look of what their contemporaries had to say about them quickly erases these false personal opinions.

xi Journalists carried with them wax sheets on which they could quickly write every word of the discussion in their own shorthand.

xii The most prominent Ionians were Homer, Socrates, Pythagoras, Euripides, Euclid, Archimedes, Hesiod, Origen, Didymos, Äsop, Sappho, and Democritus.

xiii Examples of Dorians: Pausanias, Aristophanes, Aristotle.

xiv For the Ionians, the earth was not the real home of man, but rather a testing and learning ground enabling him to relearn the Olympian laws, making Olympian virtues his own again after having lost them during his fall into Hades. They believed that they would continue to return to earth until they had fully achieved this goal. Therefore, the Ionians followed the teachings of nine daughters of Zeus and especially the Olympian Eros, next to Zeus the most good and beautiful of all the gods of Olympia. By contrast, the Dorians' Zeus is the ruler of Hades who demands from his subjects blood sacrifices. Since they do not have a spiritual view of the afterworld, their actions are quite materialistic.

xv As Professor John Nash has recently shown, a competitive environment, in which everyone does what is best for themselves and simultaneously the best for others, is far more efficient and stable than the Friedman model. This model implies that justice is superior to chaos, matching the Ionian Ideal, which is reflected both in history and nature.

xvi Johann Heinrich Pestalozzi, born in 1746, said: "The most important basis required for his future development is a child's emotional support." This was recently confirmed by modern research and published by Daniel Goleman in *Emotional Intelligence* in 1995.

xvii It is amazing today how many parents and teachers violate this basic rule. Once the child finds out if one thing they were taught was false, they begin to question everything taught to them by that person.

xviii These include Max Planck, Albert Einstein, Niels Bohr, Werner Heisenberg, Wolfgang Pauli, and Erwin Schrödinger, Nobel laureate in physics, who wrote *Nature and the Greeks*.

xix Einstein said that radioactive decay is deterministic, just like all other physical events defined since Galileo, but that we are presently unable to calculate it. The scientific community was not ready to recognize a currently immeasurable form of energy required to explain the deterministic model.

xx Florence Nightingale (founder of nursing), Johann Heinrich Pestalozzi (social reformer), Berthe Morisot (cofounder of impressionism), Maria Sibylla Merian (natural researcher and artist), Ellen Key (author of "Century of the Child"), Henry Dunant (founder of the Red Cross), John Boyd Orr (founder of FAO and recipient of the Nobel Peace Prize), Albert Schweitzer (humanitarian and doctor) Jacob and Wilhelm Grimm (linguistics and fairytales).

xxi Constantine the Great, Justinian, Julius Caesar, Napoleon Bonaparte, Richard Wagner.

xxii While the Ionians mourned the deaths of their enemies, Greece's Dorian population danced on their graves.

xxiii It was common practice to declare someone a traitor or heretic and then to rewrite or destroy everything that that person wrote. It must have been highly threatening to his power base for the Emperor Justinian personally to condemn the vast writings of Origen and anyone who even spoke his ideas. (Source: Medieval Sourcebook: Fifth Ecumenical Council: Constantinople II, 553)

xxiv The Ionians also created fine structures, but the photo below exemplifies the materialistic view of the Dorians. They thought that this Ionian temple (small building to the far left, built by their own hands in honor of their spiritual mother) was not big enough for their god Athena, so they used slave labor to build one that they thought was fitting of their god.

xxv Origen was one of the last great teachers of the Ionian culture at the school in Alexandria, before the Romans destroyed it.

Lightning Source UK Ltd.
Milton Keynes UK
UKHW010923051021
391660UK00001B/131

9 781982 270025